Kate Arnell

Six Weeks
to
Zero Waste

A simple plan for life

D0189792

CONTENTS

FOREWORD 6
INTRODUCTION 10

The Rs of Zero Waste 14
– Rule One: Refuse 15
– Rule Two: Reduce 16
– Rule Three: Reuse 18
– Rule Four: Repair 20
– Rule Five: Recycle 21
– Rule Six: Rot 23
– Rule Seven: Respond 24

HOW TO USE THIS BOOK 25

The Benefits 28
– Benefit One: Saving Money 28
– Benefit Two: Improved Health 29
– Benefit Three: Reduced Food Waste 31
– Benefit Four: More Quality Time 32
– Benefit Five: Learning New Skills 33
– Benefit Six: Living In Alignment With
    Your Values 34

Myth Busting 35
– Myth One: You Cannot Eat Meat 35
– Myth Two: You Must Be a Minimalist 36
– Myth Three: Everything You Own is
    Second-Hand 37
– Myth Four: Your Life Must Be One
    Big Compromise 38
– Myth Five: You Become a Mule 39

CHAPTER ONE:
A SIX-WEEK PLAN 40

WEEK 1 – SIMPLE TASKS, BINS & REFUSING 42
– Task One: Do the Simple Things First 43
– Task Two: Bin System 50
– Task Three: Refusing 55
– Task Four: Research 59

WEEK 2 – ASSEMBLE A ZERO-WASTE KIT 63
– Task One: The Kit 64
– Task Two: Get Out There 73

WEEK 3 – THE BATHROOM & PERSONAL CARE 82
– Task One: Tackle the Bathroom 83
– Task Two: Simplify Your Beauty Routine 91

WEEK 4 – CLEANING & GEEKING 96
– Task One: Cleaning 97
– Task Two: Geek Out 112

WEEK 5 – DECLUTTER! 115
– Task One: Decluttering 116

WEEK 6 – START COMPOSTING
& DO SOMETHING! 124
– Task One: Start Composting 125
– Task Two: Do Something! 132

CHAPTER TWO:
ZERO WASTE IN ACTION 144

The Zero-Waste Wardrobe 146
– Rule One: Buy Less! 147
– Rule Two: Choose Well 148
– Rule Three: Make It Last 151

Zero Waste at Work 153
Eating Out Without Waste 157
Family & Friends 160
Events & Celebrations 163
Travel 169
Babies & Kids 175
Pets 180

CHAPTER THREE:
USEFUL RECIPES 184

IN THE KITCHEN 186
CLEANING 198
BEAUTY PRODUCTS 206

A FINAL NOTE 212
RESOURCES 214
INDEX 218
REFERENCES 222
ACKNOWLEDGEMENTS 223

FOREWORD

In September 2013, my husband came home from work with one of the free newspapers they hand out at train stations. He pointed to an article about a family of four who lived in California. They had managed to reduce their annual trash down so much that it fitted into a quart jar (just over a litre). 'Impressive,' I thought as I marvelled at the fact that this was even possible. After reading about some of the simple ways they had managed to reduce their waste as a family, I felt inspired to find out more about the zero-waste lifestyle. I wanted to see if it was something I could embrace in my own way where I lived.

I have always been passionate about choosing organic (for the environment, the reduced pesticides and highest standards of animal welfare) but often felt pained by the amount of excessive plastic packaging it came wrapped in, especially in supermarkets where organic is heavily over-packaged to keep it separate from the non-organic produce. Every week I felt awful adding a mountain of single-use, mostly 'not currently recycled' plastic packaging waste to our bin bags. A week or so later, I visited a nearby charity shop and stumbled on a book written by the mother of the family featured in the newspaper article – *Zero Waste Home* by Bea Johnson. I took it home and read it with delight, racing through the pages and finally feeling like I could live in a way that aligned more closely with my values. I realized I didn't have to produce all of this waste week in and week out – I could take charge

and feel in control of my choices instead of simply accepting that waste was a normal part of our lives.

The more I thought about it, the more I understood that waste doesn't really exist in nature. Any 'waste' is turned into something else, something useful to another plant or creature. Waste as I knew it was a design flaw, a failure of the imagination, or someone or something not being held accountable for their actions. Waste is created by humans and I felt uneasy contributing to the growing mountain of it through my daily actions. Almost overnight, and much to my husband's surprise, I decided to embark on a zero-waste lifestyle.

There was a lot of trial and error, a lot of online searches. I had to start thinking in different ways and retrain my brain. I had lived the first 30 years of my life thinking nothing of disposing of things, no consideration for where they ended up. As I began searching for low-waste options, I started to feel increasingly frustrated. As a country we seemed so far behind others when it came to finding food available to buy without packaging, locating refills or plastic-free options.

As a result, I decided to start a blog and a YouTube channel where I shared my journey – what worked and what didn't.

My aim was to not only be a point of reference for people looking to reduce their waste but also present it in a fun, entertaining and guilt-free way. I hoped people would enjoy my content whether they cared about their waste or not. I had previously worked as a TV presenter and my last job was writer and host of *Anglophenia*, a show for the BBC America YouTube channel. On the show I explained the quirky differences between the USA and UK, all delivered with a touch of humour. Some of the videos, such as *How to Swear Like a Brit*, went viral and I gathered a strong following on YouTube. My hope was that people who enjoyed those videos would hop over to my personal channel to watch me chat about how I shop without packaging.

I'm not a hippie, I live in central London, I enjoy a bath and I wash my laundry on a hotter temperature than is recommended (more on that later). The zero-waste lifestyle is a different journey for everyone, and while waste is a huge problem for the planet, berating people into doing something never works. My aim was to show that it didn't have to be 'perfect' and if one or two people started refilling their liquid soap instead of buying a new bottle each month, or remembering their reusable water bottle and cloth bags before leaving the house, then I felt I was having a positive impact. It's been exciting to see so many influencers, bloggers and YouTubers talking about zero waste and that it has become a global movement.

I'll admit that it all seemed a little intimidating at first, especially several years ago when the majority of people had little idea of our plastic pollution problems or wider issues with waste. I have found that trying to maintain your current lifestyle exactly as it is while attempting to reduce your waste can be frustrating and leave you feeling like you're failing. Accepting that there will need to be some adaptability, some changes in order to make it work, is key. For example, I vividly remember going into a supermarket and asking at the meat counter if they could put some chicken straight into my own container without plastic. The man mumbled something about 'health and safety/company policy' and I walked away (without any chicken) realizing I had to make some lifestyle changes. Shopping at supermarkets wasn't going to work if I wanted to quit plastic packaging. As a result, I now support local shops that sell produce such as meat, cheese, beer, wine, oil and dry goods without packaging or as refills, and they are all happy to help support my low-waste efforts.

Today, I am happy to say that the UK has come along leaps and bounds in the past couple of years and we seem to have a dedicated 'zero-waste store' popping up somewhere in the country each week. Even leading supermarkets are displaying signs in their stores encouraging people to bring their own reusable containers to the deli, cheese and meat counters, as well as remembering to bring their reusable bags. The media has done an incredible job of keeping the conversation around waste going and, as a result, we have governments around the world implementing or talking about taxes on disposable plastics and looking at better ways to hold businesses to account for their wasteful ways. I wish I could tell you that I can fit my annual trash into a small jar like some of the zero-waste-lifestyle advocates out there. But due to where I live, my limited access to composting and the fact that sometimes non-recyclable plastic packaging accidentally or unintentionally makes its way into my home, I still create some waste. I'm not perfect and I don't believe anyone should try to be. But what is noticeably different since embarking on this lifestyle is not only the dramatic reduction in the amount of waste I produce but also the type of waste I make. The majority of it is food scraps (fear not, I'm bothering my council about introducing kerbside compost collections and they're finally trialling it out on a few streets in my area). It is a fraction of what I used to throw out – down from two large plastic bin bags a week to one small paper bag every two weeks.

By voting for the kind of world we want with every penny spent, being considered about every choice made and action taken, making changes – no matter how small – in our daily routines, we can quickly begin to see results. I've also found that there's nothing quite like living in alignment with your values – our choices don't have to feel like life is one big compromise.

INTRODUCTION

In recent years, thanks to social media and programmes such as *Blue Planet II*, people's awareness of plastic has grown, with a focus on the single-use, disposable kind being a huge area of concern. Studies are showing just how pervasive the material is, with reports of human-related debris (99.8 per cent of which was plastic) washing up on Henderson Island in the South Pacific, an uninhabited island in one of the most remote parts of the world.[1] Microfibres shed from clothing in the wash and microplastics – pieces of plastic that have been broken down into smaller and smaller particles over time in the environment – are found to be contaminating both our food chain[2] and the majority of tap and bottled water around the world.[3]

But, for me, a zero-waste lifestyle goes beyond avoiding single-use plastics and instead delves into all areas of unnecessary waste we unwittingly create each day. Products are becoming increasingly over-packaged, and much of it is unnecessary. Simply swapping one packaging material (such as plastic) for another (glass, metal, paper, card) continues to encourage our disposable and over-packaged habits while further draining resources. Sometimes products

packaged this way will be the best choice and we have no option, but very often the simplest and most sustainable solution is zero packaging.

Like many, I felt overwhelmed by the information out there when it came to statistics about our waste and the complicated and ineffective systems we have created around it. The main feedback I get from people is that the waste problem seems so enormous that they don't know where or how to start taking action. And even if they do, will their actions matter? I believe that once we are aware of the problem, one of the most empowering things we can do as individuals is take action over the things and habits in our own lives. While we need governments and businesses to tackle waste on a large scale in order to drive dramatic change, it can often seem like we're waiting forever to see the changes we desire come into play.

LIQUID SOAP

SHAMPOO

CONDITIONER

My hope is that this book will introduce the basics and set the stage to help you kickstart your journey towards less wasteful habits. This is a lifestyle book so you'll find very few facts and statistics. Personally, I find that they do little more than leave people feeling paralysed by the sheer scale of the problem or too confused to care. My aim is to be a positive reminder that our personal actions matter and I believe that a book about creating positive changes in habits is far more effective than a scaremongering, fact-heavy tome. You've got Google for that!

I've found that within the world of zero waste, there is a lot of focus on making everything from scratch or choosing alternatives that feel a little too 'crunchy' for my liking. Some people will love the idea of growing their own bathroom loofah, foraging horse chestnuts to use instead of laundry powder or making their own sanitary towels. But in all honesty, I've never done any of these things and I can't imagine my mother, sister-in-law or best friends growing their own loofah any time soon.

I have written this book with close friends and family in mind. I wanted to create an easy-to-follow, step-by-step guide to adopting a zero-waste lifestyle, which focuses on simple habit swaps first and introduces ways in which to reduce waste in various parts of everyday life.

Take a free jar to get you started

What the Heck Does Zero Waste Mean?

A zero-waste lifestyle can mean different things to different people. It originally began as an industry term but has since been adopted by those who are keen to reduce the amount of waste they produce in their daily lives. Essentially, producing no waste at all is the goal but most people who live a zero-waste lifestyle accept that it is almost impossible in a system led by convenience and a culture based on disposability. For most, it means taking a simpler and more considered approach to life, embracing habit changes and reusable alternatives to disposables. I'm generally more curious about the world in which we live and have loved reading and researching topics relating to waste, plastics and the environment. Each person will interpret the zero-waste lifestyle a little differently and that's okay. Enjoy discovering what it means to you and finding your sustainable sweet spot when it comes to reducing your waste.

The Rs of Zero Waste

Zero-waste pioneer Bea Johnson outlines 'Five Rs' – **Refuse, Reduce, Reuse, Recycle, Rot** – which she proposes following in order, as an effective way of staying on track with the zero-waste lifestyle. I have decided to expand on these a little to include two extra Rs (Repair and Respond), which I felt were important additions to making the zero-waste lifestyle a success. Notice how recycling is almost a last resort. By refusing, reducing, reusing and repairing first, the amount of recycling to be done should be minimal.

1 REFUSE

Refuse what you don't need. Say 'no thanks' to freebies, gifts, flyers, samples, plastic bags, straws, junk mail, business cards (take a photo instead), napkins, tissues, receipts, goodie bags. By stopping items from coming into our lives we do not have to waste time and energy storing then decluttering them later on. Every time we accept a freebie, we're saying 'please create more!'. The more we refuse, the more we are voting for the kind of non-disposable world we want. It can feel a little awkward at first, but find a phrase that works for you. A simple 'no thanks, I'm good' or 'you know what, I'm okay' is enough and there's no need to rant at someone about their wasteful practices. You may also feel that your simple action of refusing a receipt, even if one is printed automatically, is pointless but the more people who refuse them, the more a retailer will realize they have a bin full of unwanted receipts and perhaps emailing them instead would save the business money. Do not underestimate the power of refusing and the more you practise, the more natural it will become. And it's free!

2 REDUCE

Reduce what you do need. Less is more. By simplifying what I truly need I also feel less stressed and, over time, I've saved money. It also means I create less waste, having reduced the need for many disposables – either by finding reusable alternatives or something that is multipurpose – or realizing I don't actually need it. Everyone's needs are different, so reducing is quite a personal matter. For someone who bakes a lot, an assortment of kitchen gadgets may be necessary. Assess what is used and what sits forgotten at the back of the cupboard to help decide what should stay and what should go.

By reducing the items we own, we look to rent or borrow instead of buying when we do need something. For example, my husband and I went wild camping for a night with some friends a couple of years ago. Instead of buying a tent, backpacks and sleeping bags for one night, we simply asked friends on Facebook if we could borrow theirs. We managed to borrow everything we needed for the night and loved not having to store it away in our tiny flat once we returned.

Reducing our possessions also means we have boosted the second-hand market by donating or selling items. There is

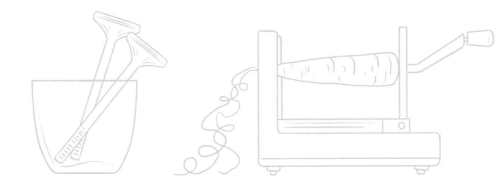

a growing number of websites and apps to help make selling items quick and easy, and it's nice to make a little extra money on the side. Try to reduce items responsibly by donating, selling or recycling as much as possible. Some items will be beyond saving, but it can be worth putting them on a site such as Freecycle – someone may be looking for just one working part or a random item for an art project. One man's trash is another man's treasure as they say!

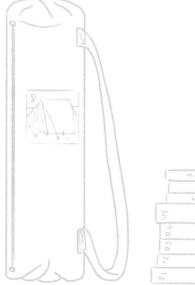

3 Reuse

Reuse by replacing disposables with reusables. We're lucky that there are now reusable alternatives to most disposables on the market. Reusing is different to recycling, as it encourages us to keep the item in its current form and at its highest value without the need for a process to break it down and build it up again. Reusing is actually my favourite 'R' in the world of zero waste. It is the turning point at which we let go of our disposables and start to embrace reusable alternatives which will be with us for the long term.

There can be an upfront cost associated with reusables which may put some people off but personally I have found that by investing in reusable items I love, I am far more likely to remember to use them and I have saved money over time. For example, one of my earliest reusable purchases was a menstrual cup to replace disposable sanitary pads and tampons. It cost me £22 but it will last me 10 years. It's estimated that the average menstruating person spends between £5 and £13 each month on tampons and sanitary items. Even if we take the lowest amount, my menstrual cup will

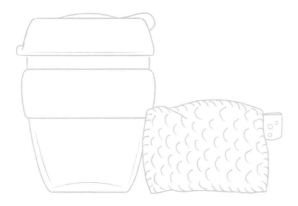

have paid for itself within the first five months, meaning that every month after that I make a saving for the next decade. Remembering a reusable water bottle instead of purchasing disposables on the go is another great example of how savings can really add up through the year. But the biggest win of all in my eyes is the amount of waste saved. By choosing reusables instead of disposables, we are creating more sustainable habits.

Choosing reusables doesn't have to be expensive, and often we have suitable items sitting in our cupboards at home.

But try to resist hoarding every reusable item possible, especially if it's not needed. Squirreling away 50 glass jars when you only really need 20 is a waste and means others cannot benefit from the materials. By refusing and reducing first, there will be fewer items that need reusing. Shopping second-hand, borrowing or renting are all great ways to encourage reuse.

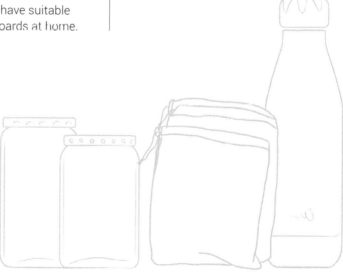

4 REPAIR

Repair and care for items to keep them in use longer. I could have easily added 'repair' to the section on 'reuse' but I felt it deserved its own paragraph as I firmly believe it plays a vital role in changing our relationship with stuff. Sadly, it is often more affordable to buy a new item instead of having an old one repaired and there are fewer businesses offering a repair service. But where possible, I choose to invest in items that come with repairability built into their design. For example, my jeans are not only made from organic cotton, but they also come with a free repairs service for life. Investing in items that can be repaired not only supports businesses that are taking responsibility for their products, but often means we can save money in the long term as well as resources.

If your sewing skills are anything like mine, then using repair services is a great idea as it means we are supporting skilled locals and keeping their craft alive. Instead of investing in a new winter coat each year, I like to take mine to the local tailor and have the lining replaced if torn. I also believe that repairing builds a magical kind of loyalty to our things. By caring for them, we are far more likely to love them for longer.

In the near future, I would like to see all companies offer repairs as part of their business model. This would boost customer loyalty and mean that companies actually take responsibility for their products. They would all begin to design with repairability in mind.

5 RECYCLE

Recycle what you cannot refuse, reduce, reuse or repair. While many people promote recycling more as the solution to our wasteful ways, we should really aim to recycle LESS. I do believe that recycling plays a vital role in reclaiming materials and keeping them in use, but too often it is used as the first port of call when actually we should look to reduce our disposable habits and the amount of packaging that comes with it. Not all recycling is created equal either. Plastics, for example, often end up getting 'downcycled', meaning they are turned into a lesser-quality material that cannot be recycled – essentially recycling delays it from landfill but it will still end up there eventually. Aluminium and glass, on the other hand, can both be recycled infinitely without losing quality while card and paper can be recycled several times and then composted. So if I must buy something with packaging, I look for materials such as metal, glass and cardboard which have a higher chance of being made into a similar product.

Purchasing products made using recycled materials is a great way to create demand for recycled materials. If there is no demand, then the materials have little value and may end up being wasted regardless of whether or not they can technically be recycled. But be careful when it comes to products made from recycled plastic. This may seem like a nice way to close the loop but it often creates more problems down the line. For example, I am seeing more and more clothing items proudly stating they are made from recycled beach plastics. Not a bad idea until you read that those materials will shed tiny plastic microfibres in the washing machine. Those microfibres have been shown to end up in our food chain and tap water, as they slip through filters and out into the ocean where they are consumed by sea life.[4] Not so great after all! Also consider if the item made from recycled materials can in fact be recycled itself. Mixing materials that cannot be separated means the item will probably end up in landfill.

Inevitably, there will always be a need to recycle, even in the zero-waste lifestyle, but I've found our recycling bin only needs emptying once a month compared to once a week. Recycling systems differ from place to place – sometimes even neighbouring areas collect completely different materials, with one accepting all recyclables in a single container and another requiring you to seperate them first. Familiarize yourself with what is accepted in your local kerbside collection service; if there are items that are not collected, find out if they can be taken to a recycling facility nearby or sent to a specialist company. For example, when decluttering I sent wine bottle corks and old scratched CDs to companies who actively recycle them into new products. Items such as cooking oil, metal razor

blades and batteries (although I use rechargeable ones now) all have to be saved and taken to a larger recycling facility near me.

It's important to remember that there are still many countries where recycling systems do not exist. Thankfully, there are charities who are working to establish recycling facilities in countries where there is little or no provision for recycling. Through their work, they have helped to recover precious materials, improve the local environment and create jobs simply through building recycling systems.

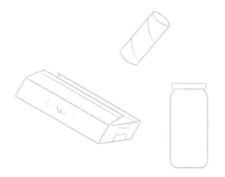

6 ROT

Rot the rest! Composting is one of those things I wish I had started sooner. I opted for an indoor worm bin system but I'll talk later about the various options available (see page 128). There is something extremely satisfying about closing the loop and, with composting, you can watch it happen before your very eyes and see the result. Humble vegetable peelings and shredded cardboard egg cartons are magically turned into nutrient-rich feed for plants within a matter of weeks.

You may even have a kerbside food waste collection service available to you. If so, use it! It can be surprising to see just how little waste we actually produce once we start composting. While my worm bin is limited in what it can take (no meat, dairy products or citrus peels, for example), it has still managed to dramatically reduce the majority of our food waste.

Some of the items I regularly add to our worm bin include: coffee grounds, tea leaves (many tea bags contain plastic so double-check before composting), hair, fruit and vegetable scraps, washed egg shells, cardboard egg cartons (although I reuse these to buy loose eggs most of the time), cleaned waxed paper (from butter), certified home-compostable cellophane such as Natureflex (look for the certified home-compostable label) and matches.

7 RESPOND

Respond with feedback. I will talk more on this later in the book (see pages 132–42) as it's one of the actionable steps but, for now, I want you to know that taking the time to communicate with a company about their packaging is one of the most empowering things we can do as consumers and citizens. Writing, tweeting or emailing a company takes little time and can have a huge impact. Your voice matters, so feel empowered to say something and, if necessary, return any unwanted packaging to be disposed of 'responsibly'.

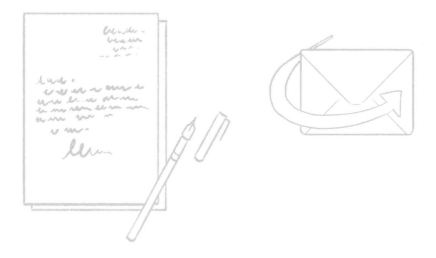

HOW TO USE THIS BOOK

This book should act as a guide (and be kept and referred to from time to time, or passed along to friends once you no longer feel you need it), starting with the simpler, 'low-hanging fruit' actions and gradually working towards the tougher, larger tasks. Whether it does indeed take you six weeks, or it actually takes six months or six years, going zero waste doesn't happen overnight and for the majority of us, creating 'zero' waste is not entirely possible, depending on what we have available to us. I want this book to be a reassuring voice that removes any guilt and encourages folks to do the best they can in that moment and focus on the positive actions to be taken.

Throughout this book, there will be examples and suggestions which work well for me, but I want the core focus to be on the process of embracing change, encouraging you to think outside the box, get creative and introduce some new habits which, once in place, will seem like second nature and suit your lifestyle. This will be by trial and error.

Having lived this lifestyle for several years, I want to dispel any myths that it is extreme, difficult or a compromise. Or that it should be taken literally. It's about finding what works for you and the 'zero' is something to work towards – the elusive carrot that dangles just out of reach but keeps you motivated enough to not settle at simply recycling a little better. In our linear system of take, make, throw, it can be almost impossible to create zero waste. Not all waste is created equal and I think it's good to consider the type of waste we produce too. Personally, I like the term 'zero waste' as it encourages me to think 'What else can I do?' If you prefer 'low waste' or 'a little less waste', then use it. Whatever works for you!

We all live different lives with varying needs so what works for me in rainy old London, might not be the same for someone living in a heat wave on the other side of the world. I want to encourage you to start thinking locally, use what systems are in place where you live and create your own rule book which aligns with your values, your living situation and your budget. There is no one-size-fits-all approach, no right or wrong, no rules to be broken. This is your journey and you decide how far you want to go.

This book is divided into four main parts. First, you'll find the actions to be taken over the course of six weeks (or whatever time frame you feel is appropriate) to encourage new waste-saving habits.

Next up, I show you zero waste in action. This gives examples of how to incorporate zero waste into different scenarios, such as spending time with friends and family, events and travel. In the third section, I've gathered all of my favourite recipes for food, cleaning and beauty. Finally, you'll find a directory of products, services and resources you may find useful.

Zero-Waste Terminology

Bulk I had always thought of bulk as being an enormous quantity of something, like giant tubs of mayonnaise or huge sacks of brown rice. And to many people, this is what bulk means. But I later discovered that it can also mean buying items such as dry goods, oils, wines and vinegars without packaging. I call this buying from bulk as opposed to buying in bulk. For those who don't have access to a bulk/refill section, buying in bulk could be the next best thing if space and storage aren't limited. But encouraging people to bring their own containers and refill is preferable as it means we only buy what we need, create new consumer habits and an economy based on refilling. It's exciting to see more and more well-known brands offering refills as part of their service, as well as bulk bin dispensers appearing in supermarkets.

Tare The 'tare' is the weight of an empty container. When bringing your own jars and cloth bags to a store, most servers will be able to tare the container on their scales before filling it. At many bulk stores, you can often weigh the empty container yourself and simply write the tare weight clearly on the outside for the cashier to see. Either way, they will deduct the weight of the container from the total weight so you only pay for what is inside. Some stores may not be able to do this (although rarely); in which case, I use cloth bags where the weight is minimal and won't add much to the total cost. Sometimes the store will simply give you a discount for bringing a reusable.

The Benefits

While the zero-waste lifestyle focuses on reducing personal waste,
I have been delighted to discover that as a result of living this way,
I have also saved money, improved my health, built my confidence and
I finally feel like I'm living in alignment with my values. At the end of the
day, if someone said that the way I live now had no impact whatsoever
on the world's waste or environmental issues, I would still continue to
live this way. It's simpler, easier and far more fulfilling than trying to
keep up with the rat race of convenience.

BENEFIT 1

Saving Money

No longer buying magazines, expensive cleaning products, disposable sanitary products, kitchen roll, aluminium foil and clingfilm, and choosing second-hand items instead of new, all adds up to some huge savings over time. In many cases, buying unpackaged food works out to be a lot more affordable than the packaged equivalent. However, food is one area where this lifestyle may at first seem a little more expensive. But remember, cheap food is cheap for a reason. And even if you end up spending a little more, the amount of money not being spent in other areas still means that the zero-waste lifestyle as a whole is far more cost effective. The zero-waste lifestyle also encourages you to use up every bit of food possible, as food waste is still waste, even if it can be composted and turned into a nourishing soil addition at the end. It's far better to gain an extra meal or snack from it first.

IMPROVED HEALTH

One of the most unexpected side effects of living a zero-waste lifestyle for me was my improved health. Not that I was sickly before, but I have certainly noticed a dramatic improvement in my sense of smell as a result of reducing my exposure to chemical cleaning products, synthetic perfumes and personal care items filled with fragrance. I also rarely get colds or flu any more. My husband has noticed a difference too and we both find that synthetic chemical-laden cleaning products give us headaches and him a tight chest. In fact, when staying with relatives recently in the middle of the countryside, surrounded by fresh air, he struggled to breathe due to the heavy-duty cleaning products used in their home. When he looked at the ingredients in the products he was shocked to discover that they were all linked to respiratory issues.

How sad that our bodies were previously numb to the ill effects of these chemicals.

The term 'fragrance' can actually be a way for companies to hide what is truly in their products as their scent is considered an industry secret. We honestly have no idea what we're slathering onto our bodies or using in our homes every day.

We have simplified our cleaning products to white vinegar, bicarbonate of soda and a washing up liquid refill and our personal care products consist of all-natural essentials. We do not have scented candles, air fresheners or products that contain any synthetic scent such as lotions. And the only perfume I occasionally wear is made from 100 per cent certified organic alcohol and essential oils (and can be refilled).

We also tend to cook more from scratch with the majority of what we eat being real food which is seasonal, local and mostly grown without synthetic pesticides.

UK government testing has found that almost half of our food contains pesticide residues[5] – in many cases the residues are made up of more than one pesticide. I don't feel comfortable exposing myself to these three times a day, every day, no matter how safe the experts claim them to be. As most takeaways and ready meals come heavily packaged, we generally don't eat them which means we're consuming far fewer nasties such as preservatives, artificial flavours, food colourings, flavour enhancers and hidden sugars.

A recent study by Australian researchers has even found links between the chemicals found in plastic food packaging and increased incidences of cardiovascular disease, type-2 diabetes and high blood pressure in men.[6] That's another good reason to reduce the amount of packaged foods, especially those that come in plastic, in our daily lives.

By choosing items made from natural materials or second-hand, we are also reducing our exposure to harmful chemicals that off-gas in our homes.[7]

WASHING UP LIQUID

VINEGAR

REDUCED FOOD WASTE

Some folks like to argue that packaging helps fight food waste, stopping it wilting or rotting during transit. Personally, I disagree. Instead I believe the packaging enables an unsustainable system which promotes flying in foods from far-off lands and often leads to large amounts of food waste, either after opening at home or by being tossed into the bins behind supermarkets as they can no longer sell them.

According to figures from the UK Waste and Resources Action Programme (WRAP), Britons throw away 40 per cent of bagged salad bought in the UK. What a waste! Not only have these leaves been picked in another country, packaged in single-use plastic filled with nitrogen gas and flown across the world, they then wilt within a day or two of sitting in our fridges and subsequently get thrown out. Food packaging is designed to protect the food sellers, not the food itself. Far better to buy a head or two of locally grown salad leaves as they will not only last longer unpackaged in the fridge, but they are also likely to stretch across many different meals (as well as taste better too!).

Food packaging also comes with over-cautious 'best before' dates which encourages food waste. Half of the food we throw away can actually still be eaten and, according to the National Resource Defense Council, 'sell by' dates on food products aren't a reliable way of indicating if food is even safe to eat or not. I used to be that person who lived by 'best before' dates, throwing out anything that was a day over its 'expiry'. Now though, I rely on my senses – touch, smell and sight – to discover if something is truly destined for the compost bin and I'm delighted to say, in the last five years, I haven't fallen ill with food poisoning once. It has also helped me reconnect with food, appreciate what is in season and understand how long certain foods last.

More Quality Time

Most people assume that a zero-waste lifestyle is going to be more inconvenient and generally time consuming. And honestly, it may seem this way at first, especially when introducing new habits and figuring out where to buy groceries, how to grab lunch on the go and sourcing plastic-free beauty products. But once things are in place, I've found that this lifestyle has freed up a lot of time and comes with the added bonus that the time spent doing chores is far more enjoyable. Cleaning is generally easier thanks to less clutter, simple cleaning products and taking a more relaxed approach.

I no longer waste away my Saturday afternoon mindlessly shopping for things I don't need as a way to pass the time. Instead, I enjoy eating out with friends and family, learning new skills (bee keeping, foraging, spoon carving, learning the harmonica!) and going on walks in the country with my husband.

I rarely have to sort through piles of receipts (except for my annual tax return), junk mail (although some still finds its way through my letterbox, but only occasionally), or piles of paper documents (most are available online).

It has also made me more organized, as thinking ahead and planning a little is not only a great way of using time efficiently but also means I feel generally calmer and in control.

BENEFIT
5

Learning New Skills

Since embracing a zero-waste lifestyle, my ability to make and do things has improved. I now have a better understanding of how things are made.

My communication skills have also improved thanks to a zero-waste lifestyle. I'm a naturally shy person and used to find it painful to ask someone in a shop to do something like cut just a slice of cheese, out of a fear of inconveniencing them. Going zero waste has encouraged me to step outside of my comfort zone and ask the server at the deli counter if they could cut me a piece of cheese and put it straight in my cloth bag. This simple habit change has resulted in me feeling generally more confident and building some lovely relationships with people I see on a weekly basis.

I have also become more curious about the world in general and have rediscovered a love of learning and reading as a result. If you enjoy learning new skills and a sense of achievement then the zero-waste lifestyle will certainly be for you.

Living in Alignment with Your Values

For so long I felt I was living a life of compromises. I hated buying plastic-packaged produce, but didn't understand that there was an alternative way to operate. I knew the toxic-chemical-laden beauty and cleaning products I was using probably weren't good for my health. But I was unsure how to change or what the other options were. By refusing unnecessary packaging, not engaging in the system of disposability and choosing to spend my money on services or things that are made or operate in a considered way that aligns with my own values gives me a great sense of empowerment and freedom.

I've noticed most people take a real sense of pride when remembering to use their reusable coffee cup or refusing a plastic bag. The feel-good factor is a little addictive.

MYTH BUSTING

MYTH
1

YOU CANNOT EAT MEAT

When I started sharing my zero-waste journey with the wider world, I was surprised to find comments from people telling me that my efforts didn't matter if I continued to eat meat. Everyone and anyone will have an opinion about what you 'should' be doing. But in the end, it's up to you. For example, after 13 years of being vegetarian, my body was finally shutting down. I was exhausted, depleted and constantly hungry. Every cell in my body was crying out for meat and oily fish and I've been healthier and happier ever since I started eating animal products again. Please do not feel bullied or guilted into eating a certain way. What and how you eat is entirely up to you and if it's a topic you're interested in, I encourage you to do some reading around it, question the 'facts' and listen to your body.

The more I read about our food system and the environment, the more I believe our true focus should be on the health of our soils, and animals play a crucial role in helping to build healthy soils, which in turn can sequester carbon as well as produce nutritious foods without the need for chemical inputs. The issue isn't animals. The issue is the systems we use to farm them. I could talk about this for hours, so I will simply say, be strong and do what is right for your body, budget and climate.

MYTH 2

YOU MUST BE A MINIMALIST

One common myth is that in order to live zero waste, you must be a minimalist. While the lifestyle encourages you to consider what you bring into your life, and generally leans towards being more minimalist, it is not a requirement. For some, being surrounded by the things they cherish brings comfort. The problem is when our stuff becomes 'stuffocating' and we stop enjoying the things that once gave us joy. Instead they become time-consuming chores, adding to the stress in our lives. The real danger is when we rely on buying stuff to fill emotional holes, suppress feelings of inadequacy or as a distraction to avoid boredom.

There will be many pictures on social media of minimalist interiors associated with a zero-waste lifestyle but do what works for you. I tried simplifying to a point beyond my comfort zone in the beginning and felt a little resentful at only having one wooden spoon to stir my cooking!

EVERYTHING YOU OWN IS SECOND-HAND

The majority of people living a zero-waste lifestyle promote buying second-hand where possible. And I tend to agree but I feel this isn't always a realistic option for everyone. In my humble opinion, there is nothing wrong with purchasing something new, as long as it has been a considered purchase, it is made by a company who are doing things better and the item can be easily repaired or recycled at the end of its life. The true issue is in the rate of our shopping habits and the sheer volume of new items we buy. Fast fashion, for example, encourages us to purchase a new outfit every week. Often the clothing is made from cheap, synthetic fabrics that are destructive to the environment both during manufacture and once they've been thrown away. The false affordability of fast fashion also means it is far simpler for people to go out and buy a replacement than mend the items they already own.

Continuing to shop at this rate, even if we are purchasing second-hand or consciously made items, is unsustainable and a wardrobe filled with clothing made from organic materials that aren't being worn is still a waste of precious resources.

Reducing the amount of stuff we have is essential but reducing the frequency of purchases is just as important. If you are buying new, buy to last. I like to use my toaster as the perfect example. It's made in the UK (it even has the name of the person who assembled it on the bottom – thanks Liam!) and is one of the most durable toasters on the market. In the rare case that it does stop working, it can be easily repaired by the company, unlike the majority of toasters on the market which are essentially designed for landfill once they stop working. We bought it new and I have no regrets. Please do not feel guilty when buying new. Try, instead, to consider how needed the item is in the first place, what it is made from, who made it and where it will end up.

YOUR LIFE MUST BE ONE BIG COMPROMISE

Another assumption about zero-waste living is that it is one big compromise. That by depriving ourselves of the overwhelming choices modern life offers, we are somehow missing out. All I can say is that since adopting this way of living, I do not feel I am lacking in anything and in fact feel I have gained so much in the form of knowledge, experiences, skills and confidence. Living with less has meant living more.

YOU BECOME A MULE

Finally, people often assume that because I bring reusables with me, I must be carting around a huge bag, filled with every reusable possible for those just-in-case scenarios 24/7. I have even seen posts on social media of people carrying their zero-waste 'kits' with them, which consist of a water bottle, a coffee cup, cloth bags, hankies, reusable straws, metal sporks or a bamboo cutlery set to name a few. In reality, I usually have a couple of reusable cloth bags stuffed in a pocket or my bag (perfect for grabbing a croissant on the go, making a spontaneous bulk purchase or simply using in lieu of a napkin) and a reusable water bottle. That's it.

I like to go with the flow and if I don't have a suitable reusable to hand, I try to think creatively. I once used my water bottle to buy sausages from the butcher as I'd left the house in a hurry and realized later that I needed to buy some food for the evening. The butcher loved the challenge of squeezing eight sausages into my empty water bottle and started singing 'sausage in a bottle' to the tune of *Message in a Bottle* (by rock band The Police) as I thanked him and waved goodbye. I appreciate some people are more comfortable going with the flow than others, but just do your best and don't be afraid to give it a go. Not only is it rewarding, it can also be a wonderful conversation starter and may even make someone's day. I like to think the butcher still talks of the sausage-in-a-bottle challenge to this day.

A SIX-WEEK
PLAN

In this chapter I'll be setting you weekly tasks to help you on your zero-waste journey. If you find there is too much to do in one week (or not enough!), then you can of course go at a pace that is comfortable for you. This isn't a race or a quick fix and it's not about only producing enough waste to fill a quart jar (although it could happen in time). I want you to start making long-lasting, sustainable changes that work for you and your lifestyle, and which will become second nature to you.

Leave perfection at the door and do what you can. Even if you only adopt a few of the habits and reusables, you'll be taking positive actions which will likely build over time. Now go forth, and waste less!

WEEK

SIMPLE TASKS, BINS & REFUSING

When I first embarked on my zero-waste journey I mistakenly started by decluttering EVERYTHING, only to discover later on that there were some items I actually still needed and wished I hadn't donated to the charity shop. Also, the time and energy it takes to declutter as a first step can seem so overwhelming that it instantly puts many people off. Being a minimalist isn't essential to living this lifestyle.

So, instead of emptying every drawer, cupboard and closet in your first week of adopting this lifestyle, try focusing on the easy things to build confidence, implementing a minimized bin system, practising new habits, and locating stores and services nearby where you can buy loose products and refills.

DO THE SIMPLE THINGS FIRST

THE LOWDOWN

Sit down at the computer and start tackling some easy wins. Once set up, they are almost entirely forgotten about. Try not to think of it as admin, but as an opportunity to free your future self from waste and the chore of dealing with it. Take some time to consider what you could achieve in the space of an hour while at your computer and write a list to tick off as you go.

TO DO

The following ideas might sound like small, insignificant changes but they really do add up. For example, my brother recently swapped to a regular delivery of tree-free toilet roll wrapped in paper, started using his local authority's food waste collection and began bringing reusable metal containers to his butcher to put the meat straight in. He went from producing three bin liners full of waste per week, to one. And those were the only changes he made.

BEFORE YOU START

Cancel magazine subscriptions. I rarely have time to read them and I can always go digital. Simply cancel the monthly payment.

Switch to a green energy supplier. This may not seem like an obvious waste-saving action as you don't tend to notice it at home, but the wider impact is huge.

Register with your local library to join the sharing economy and have access to books, magazines, newspapers, printing and more.

Sign up to a music and video streaming service to replace physical CDs and DVDs.

Cancel phone directories and catalogues.

Switch to paper-free bank statements and bills.

simple first steps

1 **Set up a weekly milk delivery in returnable glass bottles.**
I leave the empties out to be collected, cleaned and reused each week.
If you don't have this service available to you, find milk sold in glass bottles.
If buying from a farmers' market they will often accept any returned empties
to be reused. Some larger health food stores will also accept empty milk
bottles. If you prefer plant-based milks, you could try making your own
from soaked nuts or oats, but first see if you have a local delivery
service that comes in returnable glass bottles.

2 **Sign up to a tree-free toilet paper delivery service.**
Each roll is wrapped in easy-to-recycle paper. There are also options that
come without the wrapping altogether and the rolls are delivered in a simple
cardboard box (see the Resources section, page 214).

3 **Take action to reduce the amount of junk mail.**
(See overleaf).

4 **Start using your local food waste collection service.**
Apply for the relevant caddy if needed. Alternatively, see what composting
options your local authority offers. Some have subsidized worm bins
available. If you have the ability to compost at home and could accept
waste from those who don't, add your details to a compost-sharing site
(see the Resources section, page 214).

HOW TO REDUCE JUNK MAIL

Unwanted flyers and promotional items are a huge waste of materials and quite frankly I find them extremely annoying, especially when I make a conscious effort to stop unnecessary waste entering my home. I was once shocked to find a plastic-wrapped packet of 'eco-friendly' stain remover appear through my front door.

Depending on your location, you may have to do a bit of research into how best to remove your name from automatic mail outs, but here are the steps I took to significantly reduce the amount of junk mail sitting in my mailbox.

• Make or order a 'no junk mail, flyers, free newspapers or leaflets please' sign and place it in clear view on your front door above the letter box. While this isn't foolproof and people may still choose to ignore your request, it can help to reduce the quantity of junkmail making its way into your home.

• Remove your details from marketing lists. In the UK, try 'Your Choice' by Direct Marketing Association (UK) Ltd, Royal Mail Door-To-Door Opt-Out Service and Mailing Preference Service.

• For unsolicited mail, write 'return to sender' on the envelope and pop it back in the post box. Contact the company directly and request that they remove your details from their mailing list.

• Remove your details from the open register – this is a list of people and addresses that can be bought by marketing companies and used for sending junk mail. When filling out the electoral registration form, tick the box that says 'opt out' of the open register.

• When signing up to any newsletter or buying a product or service online, ALWAYS make sure you untick the box related to physical marketing. It will say something along the lines of 'I give permission for my details to be passed on to third parties to contact me.'

GO THE EXTRA MILE!

If you have addressed most of the suggestions above then take a look at the waste that is still coming into your home and consider if there is an alternative way to tackle it. Unless you're living off-grid on a self-sufficient homestead, you're likely to still be dealing with waste.

• Start by collecting your rubbish.
Exclude any food waste as this could get gross quite quickly. Collect it in a container (or a jar) for a week, or a month, depending on how far along you are.

• Make a list of what you still throw away.
Focus on the items you think you could find alternatives for, recycle or do without. Remember, this isn't about being perfectly zero waste. If there is no viable alternative, that's okay.

• Take action – research or think outside the box.
Often there is a reusable alternative available that you might not be aware of – for example, if you're in love with disposable coffee pods, consider getting a reusable metal one and filling it with your favourite ground coffee instead. If you currently recycle your batteries, choose rechargeable ones instead. Use your network of friends and family too – perhaps someone has a compost system you can use.

- **Contact any company who packages their items.**
If you've ended up with unwanted packaging with your purchase, suggest some positive changes that the company can make (see page 138 for tips on how to write a letter).

- **Let the company know if their item breaks.**
If an item you own is broken and cannot be fixed, contact the company and convey you are disappointed in their product.

- **Ask a local shop to start offering bulk and refills.**
This is a really good idea if you're having a hard time finding a specific item. Sometimes they can easily order it in for you.

- **Repair any items you've been meaning to for some time.**
Whether it's mending a hole in the lining of a coat, replacing the sole on your shoe or fixing the broken screen on your mobile phone. Find a service that has the skills to make your items like new again (see the Resources section, page 214).

TAKING STOCK

I try to take stock every year during Plastic-Free July and I've found it to be a great catalyst for me to do a bit more as it can often be too easy to no longer notice what we're still throwing out. Sometimes, new services or products become available that we previously thought didn't exist in our area. Remember this isn't just about reducing plastic waste – look at all packaging, including recyclables too.

For example, during one Plastic-Free July:

• Recycling bags. I noted that the recycling bags provided by our kerbside collection were plastic. I tackled this by returning all the recycling bags provided (to the drop-off point at the library) and decided to collect all recyclables in a reusable bag and simply carry them to an onstreet recycling bin once a month.

• Shaving cream. I noted that my husband's shaving cream came in a plastic tub. I tackled this by finding a good shaving soap bar wrapped in paper that he really likes using (it lasts longer too).

• Beer caps. I noted that the beer caps that came with bottled beer were lined with plastic. I tackled this by finding a local store selling beer refills.

• Reusable cloths. I noted that the reusable cloths I was cleaning with were made from plastic microfibres. I tackled this by recycling the microfibre cloths and replacing them with reusable ones made from biodegradable plant-based cellulose that I can compost.

• Bottles. I noted that the glass bottle of white vinegar I use to clean with came with a plastic lid which wasn't recycled where I live. I tackled this by begging my local bulk store to start offering white vinegar refills...and they did! I have also saved plastic lids to then take to a relative's house where they are recycled in her kerbside collection or collected for charity.

BIN SYSTEM

THE LOWDOWN

Most of us have a bin in the kitchen, another in the bathroom and probably one in every bedroom too. Each of these requires time emptying and if we're keen to do the right thing, we're left fishing out potential recyclables that have been mixed in with general waste. This is an inefficient use of time and space and generally a bit of a gross task! It can also mean recyclable items get contaminated with bits of food, beauty products or compostable items which make them non-recyclable.

By removing all bins from every room, except one, we get into the habit of dealing with empty product packaging straight away and in the right way. We can no longer toss that empty shower gel bottle into a small bathroom bin along with used tissues, hair, sanitary products and cardboard toilet rolls. It now has to go straight into the one recycling bin downstairs in the kitchen.

TO DO

The simplest and most effective thing I've found is to have one location for the bins. I chose the kitchen, but a hallway or utility room could work too. Depending on where you live, some authorities will require one bin for all recyclables while others will want materials such as glass, paper/cardboard and metal to be separated. Do what your local authority requires and familiarize yourself with what they accept and in what condition it needs to be – cleaned first, squashed, unshredded?

Ultimately find a system that works best for you – the key here is to reduce the number of bins to the bare essentials; only one per category in one room of the house.

BEFORE YOU START

Choose one room in the home where the general waste, recycling and compost bins will live. No matter where you are in the home, all waste, recyclables and compostables will go in the correct bin in this room.

simple first steps

1 Set up recycling containers.

Find a container (or a few) for recyclable items that are not collected by your local kerbside collection. These are to be taken to your nearest recycling facility when full. For example, metal blades from razors, aluminium foil tops and metal lids from glass jars can all technically be recycled, but may need to be taken to a larger depot if your kerbside collection service doesn't accept these. This will need to be done less frequently but still means that recyclable materials are diverted from landfill or the incinerator.

2 Educate family or housemates.

Let everyone in the household know about the new system and show them how it works. It may sound like extra effort at first and take some time to get used to but your future selves will thank you for the reduced time spent dealing with bins in every room or telling your family/ housemates off for not recycling properly.

GO THE EXTRA MILE!

If you already have a minimal bin system in place or maybe you're producing next-to-no general waste, here are some things you could try doing to address any difficult-to-recycle items which either you can't live without or aren't sure what to do with.

• Contact your local authority.
Request a food waste collection if none currently exists.

• Look into local recycling collection schemes.
This could be for unusual items such as asthma inhalers, pens, wine corks, lightbulbs, CDs and so on.

• For extra-tricky-to-recycle items, set up a zero-waste box.
This could be done with friends and family to help split the cost (see the Resources section, page 214) or ask a local store or your work place to offer it, especially if they sell or use the difficult-to-recycle items. Ear plugs, contact lenses, used child car seats (these shouldn't be donated for health and safety reasons), used chewing gum (yes, it contains plastic!) and even cigarette butts (although, seriously, try quitting first) are all examples of things that can be collected (for a cost) and recycled.

• Could the items be reused in their current state?
Instead of recycling, could it be given away to friends in need or given a home through online sites or apps (see the Resources section, page 214). You never know, a local artist or school project may be looking for a bunch of glass jars or old CDs.

A NOTE ON BIN LINERS

One of my early frustrations was trying to find a plastic-free alternative to bin liners. To begin with I tried biodegradable bags but later found that they are still made of plastic. They have an enzyme added to make them break down faster but essentially they are still plastic. Truly compostable alternatives may biodegrade but they are likely to be sent to the incinerator or to landfill, where they will struggle to degrade due to a lack of oxygen and light.

If you can compost all food waste and don't have any wet items, then simply lining your bin with folded newspaper may be a good option (see the Resources section, page 214, for a link to a tutorial showing how to do this). However, I still produce some food waste that cannot go in my worm bin and my local authority currently doesn't offer a kerbside food waste collection so, for now, I have settled on purchasing strong paper bin liners made from tree flakes from parts of the tree that would otherwise be wasted. I order one batch a year and they sadly come in a plastic bag but I have accepted that this uses a lot less plastic than a whole bin liner a week. As soon as I have a food waste collection available to me, I will no longer need these but for now they are the best option.

REFUSING

THE LOWDOWN

Remember how our parents taught us to say 'no' to strangers? Well, I want you to channel your inner six-year-old and start saying 'no', but this time to waste. This is one of the simplest and most effective habits when living a zero-waste lifestyle. Saying 'no thanks' to things we don't really need or want may feel strange or even a bit rude at first, but every time we refuse a promotional item, an unwanted gift, a plastic bag or a single-use straw we're basically saying 'please do not create more of this product'. It saves on resources by reducing the demand for more and we end up having to declutter less in the future. Unless it's something you really, really, really need or want, try to refuse it.

TO DO

Refusing is a habit that slowly grows over time, but you can start practising it from the moment you leave the house today! Try to pre-empt things or think ahead a little, but don't worry if you forget something and end up with a disposable. It's all a learning process and you're likely to remember the next time. For example, if a waiter starts to set the table with a disposable napkin, try saying 'You know what? I'm not gonna need that, you can reuse it for someone else if you like.' Ask yourself, 'do I actually need this?' Even if it's a plastic-free alternative, sometimes it's just not needed.

BEFORE YOU START

Practise saying 'no'. Saying 'no' doesn't need to come across as impolite or awkward. Play around with different ways of refusing and find one that suits your personality. I like to add a touch of humour if I can: 'I'm good thanks, just saving the planet one plastic bag at a time,' or a simple 'nah, I'm okay thanks' works for me. My only tip is to remember that many people are still not aware of our waste problem and shouting at them for trying to give you something will come across as rude. Be kind, remember they're just doing their job and if they seem curious or insist on giving you something then you can explain a little further that you're becoming more minimalist, trying to reduce the amount of waste and clutter at home, allergic to plastic or saving the planet — whatever excuse feels right in the moment.

simple first steps

1 **Receipts.**
Over half are likely to contain the chemical BPA and cannot be recycled. Some stores can email them to you instead if you really need one.[8]

2 **Straws.**
A Jedi-like hand wave over your glass can add emphasis to this request.

3 **Takeaway coffee cups.**
Sit in and enjoy the coffee if you don't yet have a reusable.

4 **Plastic carrier bags.**
Bring your own reusables.

5 **Free tasters.**
These are usually served in single-use plastic cups.

6 **Flyers and leaflets.**
You don't need them.

7 **Business cards.**
Take a photo instead!

8 **Someone else's unwanted crap.**
Even if well-meaning friends or family offer to give you things, only accept if you actually want or need it.

9 **A paper bag for your vegetables.**
Or go loose!

10 **An extra paper napkin.**
Use your sleeve – ha, only joking! Bring a reusable napkin and return the unused disposable – if caught short, use only one and compost it at home.

GO THE EXTRA MILE!

If you already have 'no thanks' written on your t-shirt and refusing is a natural instinct, then consider other areas you could start refusing, but only if it feels appropriate.

• Gifts or goodie bags from events.
Tempting, I know, but rarely do they contain anything worth keeping.

• Free samples with an online order.
These are often non-recyclable plastic sachets. If there isn't an option to opt out when ordering, follow up with an email requesting no samples.

• Refuse to support retailers, restaurants or establishments that use wasteful practices.
Instead, champion those that make an effort to offer reusables.

RESEARCH

THE LOWDOWN

Sometimes we're completely oblivious to what we have available in our neighbourhood. It's not until we actively start looking for package-free options that we start to see them everywhere. Across the globe, there has been a surge of new zero-waste stores opening up, which has been wonderful to see but most of the time we can find unpackaged or refill options in delis, small grocery shops, butchers, farmers' markets and health food shops – heck, even the supermarket – so don't feel discouraged if there isn't a dedicated zero-waste store near you.

TO DO

This task is about seeing what's available to you. What do you have available unpackaged or in refills both locally and online? I was delighted to discover, after a quick internet search, that I had an organic greengrocer, a butcher and a cheese counter selling loose produce all under one roof and only 10 minutes walk away. There were also local places to refill wine and beer that I must have walked past and never even noticed before.

BEFORE YOU START

Get out there and explore. Look for bakeries, delis or supermarkets and make a note or take photos of what they have available without packaging.

simple first steps

1 **Start building your own go-to directory of where to find things.**
It may be tempting to ask in advance if they'd be okay with you bringing your own containers but try to resist. The less notice you give someone the more likely they are to refill your jar. When you hand it straight over with a request to 'put the olives straight in, thanks', it gives them little time to refuse or think it through. There are some great online resources for finding bulk retailers near you (see the Resources section, page 214).

2 **Get online.**
If you don't have any options in your neighbourhood or prefer the convenience of a delivery there are now several online dry goods delivery services available (see the Resources section, page 214). If you want to purchase things like oats, rice, flours, dried fruits and nuts and can't get them from bulk, then this could be a great way to support a business that is doing things differently. Often, they will use carbon-neutral shipping and minimal packaging.

3 **Look online and locally for zero-waste products.**
Buy zero-waste beauty and personal care products online (see the Resources section, page 214) or look to see if you have a local store or market selling refills or products sold in returnable or recyclable packaging

GO THE EXTRA MILE!

There's always something new to discover, and the world of zero waste is changing rapidly. A service or a product that may have been unavailable before may now exist. Use this time to stay up-to-date with your options.

• Start researching.
Think of a product or a service that you have struggled to find a waste-free alternative for and look wider. Is there a new bulk store in your neighbourhood or a plastic-free delivery service?

• Share any discoveries with others.
This can be with friends and family or those in the zero-waste community via social media.

• See if there is a meet-up group in your area and join.
If you enjoy meeting others interested in the zero-waste lifestyle, this is a great way to learn about new ideas and items.

• Research what services you have nearby.
Is there a shoe repair service?
An alterations shop?
Someone who fixes electronics?

WEEK

ASSEMBLE A ZERO - WASTE KIT

It can be tempting to wait until you have everything set up before you start getting out there and buying things like groceries without packaging. At first, it will feel odd and perhaps a little awkward but the more I practised, the more confident I felt. Especially as the feedback was often very positive.

This week is all about considering what reusables you need to help you on your way, and getting out there and putting your refilling skills to the test! Start with what feels easy and comfortable and don't be afraid to try, fail and learn as you go.

THE KIT

THE LOWDOWN

I've found that investing in some reusables to replace common disposables really helped kickstart my zero-waste lifestyle, making the whole process a lot easier. It also meant that I was excited to start using them. If you already have something at home that will do the job and you're happy using it, then please consider this option first. You don't always need to buy something new. But don't feel bad about buying a new reusable, especially if it will help you to reduce waste in the long term. There is a reusable or compostable alternative for almost everything – invest in items you will get the most use out of first.

TO DO

Decide what would work for you and your lifestyle and start searching for alternatives. The lists on the following pages are the reusables or plastic-free alternatives I have found to be useful and, while some came with an upfront cost, after five years of use I can honestly say they have all been worth it. Hopefully this will give you a little inspiration.

The lists are not exhaustive, they are simply there to inspire you – I'm certainly not saying you should rush out and buy everything right now. It can be easy to get overexcited at this point and buy a bunch of zero-waste alternatives just for the sake of buying them. I did this at the beginning and later found I really didn't need a foldable metal spork or reusable straws – a spoon from my kitchen drawer and simply going without a straw were actually far better ideas.

BEFORE YOU START

• Make a list of reusables you think you will need. Try looking at what you buy in your weekly grocery shop, and which containers would help you buy those items package-free. Look at what you purchase and dispose of regularly: takeaway coffee cups, bottled water, tea bags, makeup removing wipes, plastic packaging from grocery shopping.

• See if there is anything you already own that would do the job before buying new. Ask friends and family members if they have a specific or spare item you need. Could you make your own reusable cloth bags from an old shirt? Or reuse some shoe dust bags as cloth bags instead? Do you have any glass jars you could use instead of buying new ones?

• If buying new, invest in items that are going to be most used first, plus items that are likely to save you money. Most coffee chains offer a discount if you bring your reusable cup. Reusable sanitary products pay for themselves within a few months. Buying bottled water daily? Time to start using a reusable water bottle and save those pennies (see the Resources section, page 214 for online retailers).

• Be considered. Is the reusable item something you really need. Would simply not having it at all be the most sustainable (and most affordable!) solution?

simple first steps

1 Invest in a reusable water bottle.

This is great for when you need a drink on the go throughout the day – mine is made from stainless steel.

2 Carry reusable cloth bags.

I never leave the house without one or two of these stuffed in my pocket or bag. Fancy a croissant? Spotted something in bulk you need to buy? I simply whip out that cloth bag and fill it up! I say, 'I'll take it straight in here please – no other packaging needed, thanks.'

3 Start collecting glass jars.

These are perfect for buying deli goods in the shop and storing foods at home. I prefer the swing-top jars with a natural rubber seal and managed to find the majority of mine in charity shops but, if you're happy with any jar, repurpose ones from around the home or ask friends.

OUT & ABOUT

A lot of waste comes with our on-the-go routines: grabbing a bottle of water and coffee to go, pre-packaged sandwiches for lunch, plastic bags for any purchases. Remembering reusables can really help us to avoid unnecessary waste and, honestly, they look way cuter than disposables!

These are the items I have found most useful while out and about:

Reusable water bottle.

Reusable coffee cup. I often get a hot drink while I'm out so I bring this with me. It also doubles as a great place to store leftover food if I'm eating out and don't have a container.

Reusable cloth bags. You can either make your own from leftover material or simply buy them online or in health food stores. I have a mixture of cloth bags in different sizes, some I made and some I bought. Weigh them when empty and write or sew the weight onto the bag so, when possible, the cashier can deduct the weight and you only pay for what's inside.

Reusable napkin. I almost always have one in my pocket or bag. I choose extra-large ones so they can be fashioned into an emergency cloth bag (if unused!).

A large reusable cloth shopping bag. These are handy if I decide to buy something and I can refuse a plastic bag.

Other reusable items you may want to bring with you include:

Reusable cutlery set or spork. Great for when you are eating on the go.

Reusable container. To hold your food.

A metal, glass, silicone or bamboo straw. For if you like a straw in your drink.

GROCERIES

These are what I use for grocery shopping. Some things I use for buying fresh produce and meat each week, others I use for stocking up on dry goods and oil and vinegar refills once a month or so.

3 reusable metal airtight containers. For buying meat – one of them should be large enough to accommodate a chicken.

15–20 reusable cloth bags. All in different sizes, to be used for purchasing bread, loose dry goods such as rice, oats and coffee beans, and soft produce such as tomatoes and mushrooms.

20 reusable glass jars. I use these for buying deli items and for storing dry goods at home. I simply decant food purchased from bulk from the cloth bags into the glass jars for storage. I sometimes bring one or two with me for buying peanut butter or honey from bulk.

2 large reusable shopping bags. One for meat tins and one for everything else.

Glass bottles. I have several for refilling oils, wines and vinegars or for buying liquid cleaners.

BATHROOM & PERSONAL CARE

It can take some time to work out what you need in the bathroom, but below are some easy suggestions for reusable or plastic-free alternatives you can begin to introduce.

Refillable floss container with silk floss refills. Alternatively, pull strands of silk from a piece of material.

Wooden/bamboo toothbrush.

Glass bottles with plastic pump. These are for shampoo and conditioner refills.

Metal soap dish. This can also be used for travel.

Reusable ear pick. To replace disposable cotton buds.

Metal tweezers.

Metal nail clippers.

Reusable metal toothpick.

Washable organic cotton muslin face cloths.

Metal spice shaker. For bicarbonate of soda tooth powder.

Bidet attachment. If you're brave enough to quit toilet roll!

Reusable metal or glass containers. For storing homemade lip balm or for travelling.

Stainless steel safety razor.

Metal blades for safety razor. These come individually wrapped in paper in a cardboard box.

Menstrual cup. You can also find reusable sanitary pads, reusable tampons or reusable absorbent pants designed specifically for periods.

KITCHEN & HOMEWARES

I started by swapping the main disposable items first — such as reusable wipes to replace disposable ones, cloth napkins for paper ones, a tea infuser to replace tea bags and some glass jars for storing all the unpackaged food items I was starting to purchase.

Reusable kitchen cloths. Avoid those made from microfibres as they shed tiny plastic particles in the wash.

Wooden dish brush and bottle brush.

Metal wool scrubber/scourer.

Reusable tea strainer/infuser. Loose-leaf tea is a great option as most tea bags contain plastic.

Cloth napkins.

Glass jars. For storing dry goods.

Metal French coffee press. If you have a coffee machine that uses coffee pods, consider investing in a reusable metal version and filling it with your favourite ground coffee bought from bulk.

A NOTE ON CLEANING REUSABLES

I feel this should go without saying, but I'm going to mention it anyway. Please use common sense and good hygiene practices when using reusables. Keep containers clean and dry, and wash reusable cloth bags after each use. Replace used kitchen cloths with clean ones regularly. Ironing napkins is a great way of sterilizing them and if you use a menstrual cup, boil it in hot water with bicarbonate of soda for 10 minutes at the end of each period and store it in a clean bag ready for your next cycle.

Use the dishwasher if you have one to help sterilize glass jars and reusable containers when needed, otherwise simply wash thoroughly by hand with washing up liquid. To sterilize glass jars and lids without a dishwasher, boil them in a large pot of water for 10 minutes or place them on a tray in the oven for 30 minutes at 110°C (230°F) Gas Mark ¼ and leave to cool.

GO THE EXTRA MILE!

If you've already got your own collection of reusables sorted, look into other areas of life where you could suggest reusables instead of disposables.

- **Share how much you love certain reusable items.**
Continue to spread the word with friends,
family or on social media.

- **Contact a local school and ask them to encourage
the children to use reusable water bottles.**
At the next school fête, ask if you can set up a stall selling reusables.

- **Use your crafting skills (if you have any!).**
Make beautiful reusable items such as cloth bags or beeswax
wraps and gift them to friends or sell them.

- **Think about your workplace.**
Look into how many disposables are used and if there
are any reusable alternatives. For example, why not
propose reusable takeaway cups.

GET OUT THERE

THE LOWDOWN

Hopefully, by now, you've had a chance to research what you have available in your local area and you've invested in some reusables or dug some out from the back of your cupboard. Now it's time to venture out into the big wide world and start practising some refilling habits.

Most of the shops I frequent know the drill by now. I hand over my tins or cloth bags and they put the food straight in. I always take the time to have a little chat with the person serving me and find out how their day is going and I'm always polite. It also means I receive a few perks from time to time. Although this isn't always guaranteed, it's nice when it does happen. The butcher will throw an extra few sausages in my reusable tin or I'll get a free pain au chocolat for bringing my reusable cloth bag. Some coffee baristas have been so charmed by my reusable cup that they've let me have my coffee on the house.

It's also a great way to start a conversation. Whenever I take my reusable tins or cloth bags into a store, someone almost always says 'what a wonderful idea!' or 'where did you find those tins?'. I let my local store know that their customers seem to be interested in buying reusables similar to mine and in fact, my local farm shop now stocks them on their shelves along with signs encouraging people to bring their own. My butcher tells me others have started bringing their own egg containers to refill and he's even had some people turn up with their reusable containers for meat too. If you do become a regular and get to know the staff and owners of the store then it makes it easier to put forward suggestions. Would they consider selling some dry goods from bulk? How about offering cleaning products in refill? Don't be afraid to give them positive feedback and ideas of what you'd love to see. They're eager to please.

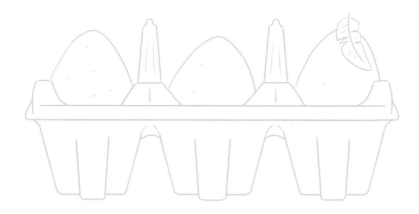

TO DO

A simple trick to get into the routine of remembering your reusables as you head out of the door is to tag them onto a habit you already have. For example, when I leave the house, I always say to myself 'phone, wallet, keys'. I now add 'water bottle and cloth bag' to the end of my chant and I've found it works surprisingly well! Find a method that works for you. If you like to pack your work bag the night before, place your reusables in it or next to it as a reminder to take them with you.

For me, one of the most enjoyable things about zero-waste grocery shopping has been supporting small, independent stores such as the greengrocer and butcher in my local area. After several years, I know them all by name, and enjoy a good chat whenever I stop by. Compared to the soulless, overlit and overpackaged aisles of the supermarket, it's a completely different experience and has made grocery shopping less of a chore and, dare I say it...fun!

BEFORE YOU START

Start planning ahead a little, it will make all the difference.

Practise remembering to bring your reusables with you. Don't feel you need to bring them all at once! Think ahead and if you know you're going to want a takeaway coffee on the way into work and grab a sandwich at lunchtime, pack your coffee cup and a reusable cloth bag.

simple first steps

1 Ask a server to put something in your own container.

Take a reusable container to your local butcher, deli or supermarket and ask them to put the item straight in, no plastic packaging.

2 Try refilling dry goods or oils at your local bulk store.

Make a list, take the correct number of cloth bags, glass jars and tins with you and start filling them up. Start with one item first to build confidence if it seems a bit overwhelming.

3 Become a regular!

Small businesses are far more likely to accommodate your requests as they really need your loyalty as a returning customer. It also means you won't have to explain yourself every time you shop.

HOW I GROCERY SHOP

The idea of grocery shopping with reusables can seem a little daunting at first. So many of us rely on the convenience of online ordering from supermarkets and having our groceries delivered to our doors but this leads to a lot of excess packaging.

It will feel odd the first few times you try asking someone to put something straight into your container or cloth bag. Be polite, use your sense of humour and be confident. Resist the urge to explain in detail why you're doing this unless someone asks. Figure out a short and sweet line that works for you. I usually say something along the lines of 'can I get that straight in here please?' and hand over the container. If they start to reach for extra paper or a plastic bag, I just add 'oh, it's okay, I don't need any extra packaging thanks. Trying to reduce our waste at home!' Here's how I grocery shop and when.

EACH WEEK

Most weeks I buy meat, fruit and veg, bread, cheese, butter, yogurt and tomato passata. I visit my local organic grocer with three reusable tins (a large one for a whole chicken and two smaller ones for whatever other meat we fancy that week), four or five reusable cloth bags, two empty egg cartons which I've saved to reuse, and two large shopping bags to carry everything home in.

I give the tins to the butcher. When ordering the meat, we enjoy a nice chat and another curious customer usually asks me where I got my containers from and exclaims what a marvellous idea it is to bring your own. I never tire of this! The butcher weighs the empty tin, places the meat inside and then deducts the weight of the tin. I only pay for what is inside (and often get a little discount for bringing my own too!).

I fill my empty egg cartons with loose eggs.

I use a large cloth bag for my loaf of bread. Or you can use an old pillowcase.

Fruits and veggies go loose into my shopping basket. Then I use the smaller reusable cloth bags for softer or delicate items such as mushroom, tomatoes and plums, anything that might squash easily.

I pick butter packaged in waxed paper. The wax paper can be washed and then composted in my worm bin (more on composting later!). The yogurt and tomato passata are the only two items I buy in glass. There is a place some distance away where I can buy yogurt in returnable glass jars, but sadly it's not that convenient for me to do it regularly. I have also tried making my own tomato passata, but I live in a tiny flat with little storage, so making enough to get me through the year just isn't realistic right now.

EACH MONTH

About once a month I make a trip to various specialist or bulk stores to stock up on things that take longer to get through. This is where they sell everything loose from bins or bulk dispensers and I can fill up on as much or as little as I need. Sometimes you will find a dedicated bulk or zero-waste store, other times you might find a bulk or refill section in a health food shop.

I take 10–15 reusable cloth bags for dry goods such as pasta, rice, oats, coffee beans, chocolate, nuts, seeds and popcorn. I use the scales to weigh each empty cloth bag and container to get the tare weight (see page 27) then fill them up.

I use glass bottles to fill up with olive oil, vinegar, washing up liquid and sometimes maple syrup.

Glass jars are used for refilling with peanut butter (freshly ground from the machine), local honey, laundry powder, herbs and loose-leaf teas.

Some bulk stores require you to take a note of the PLU number which identifies what the item is. Either write it down on a scrap of paper or do what I do and take a picture on your phone to show them at the checkout.

When buying wine or beer, I need to visit a different store and bring a glass bottle or beer growler with me. I tend to do this on a different day when I'm not carrying so many things.

Everything goes into two large reusable bags and I carry them home. I feel it's worth mentioning that I use public transport. I say this to let you know that carrying a few reusables for grocery shopping, even when filled, isn't difficult for most people. Simplifying and planning ahead a little can really make it an enjoyable task and you can cancel that gym membership too after carrying those bags!

NO BULK? NO PROBLEM!

The number of locations offering bulk has drastically increased in the last few years but some people will still find that they do not have anything sold loose or in refill form near them. Below are ideas if you don't have a bulk store available to you.

• Buy IN bulk. If you have enough storage space, you can essentially buy like a bulk store and stock up on things you know you will use, such as large bags of oats, rice, pasta, dried beans, olive oil and laundry powder.

• Look for less and better packaging – preferably glass, metal, cardboard or paper – and favour materials that are easy to recycle in your area. Farmers' markets and specialist deli stores are often good places to look.

• Get a veg box. If you don't have a farmers' market or loose veg available to you, consider signing up to a local veg box scheme. Some advertise themselves as being plastic free, but most use a lot less packaging than a supermarket. It's also a lovely way to support local food producers with the added convenience of having it delivered straight to your door.

• Simplify. How many cleaning products do we really need? Try to find multipurpose items.

• Grow your own. Herbs come in so much plastic packaging in the supermarket and are an easy place to start. If you have space, try growing some vegetables and fruits too. You could even get a couple of chickens if you're feeling plucky and fancy freshly laid eggs.

• Swap it. If you can't find a specific item sold without plastic, would something else work instead? Try using olive oil as a makeup remover, or white vinegar in place of cleaning products and fabric softener.

• Make it. For years I made pasta as I couldn't find it sold loose anywhere and I still make my own dishwasher powder as I cannot find one sold without plastic (see page 204).

• Order online. It is now possible to order dry goods online from specific plastic-free grocery stores (see the Resources section, page 214).

KEEP YOUR COOL

If someone declines to fill your reusables, don't freak out! Often
they're just worried about getting into trouble. If I've shopped
there before, I'll usually let them know that their colleagues
serve me this way all the time and it's never been an issue.
Or ask if they could check with their manager.

Worst-case scenario, accept that it's not going to happen and
consider shopping elsewhere. Following up with a polite email
to the company explaining what happened usually helps.

GO THE EXTRA MILE!

If you've got your reusables sorted, you're in the habit of shopping from bulk and you remember your reusables, here are some other ideas:

• Set up your own bulk store.
This might sound like a big task, but if there's a demand in your community, then it might be worth doing. And you'd have access to all the bulk you could ever need!

• Try hosting a zero-waste workshop.
Share how you shop and simple swaps you've made.

• Noticed a reusable product that's missing from the market?
Could you design or make it?

• Bring partners, kids or friends grocery shopping with you.
Show them how how it all works. Children will especially enjoy refilling their cloth bags.

THE BATHROOM & PERSONAL CARE

Once I had implemented the grocery shopping habits, I turned to the bathroom which was filled with multiples of shampoo, makeup, body washes and disposable razors, as well as a mountain of waste hidden in the packaging for the toilet paper and sanitary products.

I questioned what I really needed, removing any duplicates or products I knew I no longer used. I even eliminated a sponge and plastic loofah, preferring to use a bar of soap and my hands in the shower instead.

Beauty and personal care products are unique to each individual. Some experimentation is required, so please don't lose heart and remember to keep an open mind.

TACKLE THE BATHROOM

THE LOWDOWN

A bathroom should be a place of sanctuary, a place we can go to unwind from the stresses of the day and show ourselves a little love – perhaps enjoy a face mask or a little extra pampering of tired skin. The reality is that most people end up filling their bathrooms with clutter. Every available space is covered with plastic bottles of shampoo, conditioner, face cleaner, body wash, shaving cream and multiple lotions and potions, each with the promise of youthfulness thanks to the latest superfood ingredient.

How often do we consider the number of different chemicals in each of these products, including some that have been linked to hormone disruption and cancer? Not such a relaxing thought!

TO DO

This week, try swapping disposable bathroom and personal care products for durable reusable alternatives or things that can be easily composted. Overleaf are some of the products I now use as part of my personal care routine.

BEFORE YOU START

Consider realistic options you are happy to try and use the examples listed to give you some ideas.

Minimize what you actually need and look for multipurpose products. Could one bar of soap work as a hand wash, body wash, shaving soap and stain remover (see page 105)? Do you actually need a body sponge or will your hands do the job instead?

Consider using the same products for the whole household. While this may not be feasible due to everyone's unique skin and hair type, there may be some items that work for all.

simple first steps

1 Choose reusables.

Budget permitting, invest in reusable items you will use regularly and remember that some come with savings (razor blades, reusable face wipes and menstrual products all save money).

2 Try some swaps.

See which kitchen cupboard items (olive oil, honey, salt, apple cider vinegar, bicarbonate of soda) you can start using. Remember this can be a process of trial and error and if something isn't giving you the results you want, do not feel you need to compromise. There will be a suitable option out there.

3 Make sure the packaged items you are buying are sustainable.

For products that you need to buy packaged, such as face cream or body lotion, look for refills or products that come packaged in a compostable cardboard tube or recyclable metal or glass.

SOAP

I found this to be the easiest swap of all. It took some time to find a bar I absolutely love and that lathers well, but there is no shortage of soap bars to choose from out there. Personally, I look for ones that use natural ingredients and come in minimal or no packaging. I use these to replace body wash, hand wash, face wash and shaving cream.

If liquid soap is your preference, then try looking for a natural castile soap available from bulk that you can refill in store, or one sold in a glass bottle.

MOISTURIZER

I have found using olive oil bought from bulk works well as a simple moisturizer for my face. Alternative oils, often available to bulk buy, are sunflower oil, sesame oil and jojoba. Massage a few drops onto skin.

During the winter months, however, I find my skin needs something a little thicker and creamier so I use a natural face moisturizer from a brand that offers refills. I simply order a replacement and return my empty bottle to them to be cleaned and reused. It is often worth asking small brands/companies if they are happy for you to return a bottle or jar to be refilled. Your local bulk store may also have some moisturizer available from bulk.

On my body, when I remember, I either use a simple whipped body butter that I make myself (see page 208) or a body moisturizer refill from a local brand that is happy for me to return my bottle to them. Alternatively, there are plenty of body-moisturizing products in compostable cardboard tubs or tubes or glass jars or metal tins. Find what works best for your skin type.

DEODORANT

I have found that simply patting bicarbonate of soda onto my underarms keeps me smelling fresh throughout the day but this doesn't work for everyone, including my husband who develops a mild rash when he uses it. Instead, he uses a bicarb-free deodorant stick which comes in a compostable cardboard tube. Some people swear by alum stones – a natural stone which you wet and rub onto the underarm area – but I found they really didn't work for me! Some folks are lucky in that their sweat doesn't smell, so may not even need a deodorant. You can also make your own but the results are usually a little oily and can stain clothing. Keep in mind that all of these suggestions do not prevent sweat, only odour. I found my body adjusted after a couple of weeks and began to perspire a lot less as a result of quitting antiperspirant.

SUNSCREEN

Please don't make your own unless that is your business and you're a pro. The results of DIY sunscreen are unpredictable and risky. Instead, I've found options made from natural ingredients available in metal tins which can be reused or easily recycled. If you're lucky enough to have sunscreen available from a bulk store, then get refilling!

Remember that simply covering up in sensible clothing and wearing a hat can go a long way to keeping skin protected from the sun, and moderate exposure is a great source of vitamin D. I have found I am much more in tune with how long my skin can comfortably sit in the sun (about 20 minutes) before retreating to the shade.

HAIRCARE PRODUCTS

Finding a good replacement for conventional shampoo and conditioner was a bit of a challenge for me in the beginning and ended up being one of my later swaps. While some people are happy using rye flour or bicarbonate of soda instead of shampoo, I much prefer something akin to actual shampoo! This is certainly an area where a little trial and error comes in and don't be too alarmed if one product leaves you with hair like Albert Einstein.

Shampoo bars aren't for everyone but they can be worth trying, especially if you find a good one. The results can be marvellous, both from a glossy locks point of view and a reduction in waste. Follow with a conditioner (from bulk) or an apple cider vinegar rinse in place of conditioner (see page 209).

Refills are another great option. Simply take an empty bottle or two into a store or hair salon that has shampoo and conditioner refills and fill them up. I initially couldn't find a refill option near me until I asked a local organic hairdresser if I could pop in with my empty glass bottles to be refilled from their larger salon sizes. To my relief they loved the idea and I've been refilling from them ever since. There are companies that offer a refill service online. Return the bottle and they will clean it and refill it (see the Resources section, page 215).

I used to wash my hair every day which meant it got greasier much faster. While every hair type is different and some people can go for weeks without needing to shampoo, it's a good idea to see if you can extend the time between washes a little. This not only saves on products, but it also means you spend less time in the shower (saving water!) and I've found my hair and scalp to be generally happier too.

Dry shampoo can help extend the time between washes. Try a little cornstarch or arrowroot powder for lighter hair or cocoa powder for darker hair. Sprinkle from a spice shaker and brush through to absorb any grease.

HAIR REMOVAL

My personal favourite is the all-metal reusable safety razor. At first glance, it may look like it's going to shred your skin to pieces but it's called a 'safety razor' for a reason and, during the five years I have been using mine, I have only cut myself twice (in the very early days). They take a little practice and the best advice I have is to let the weight of the razor do the work (don't press down!) and simply guide it along your skin. My husband (without any encouragement from me, I should add) picked mine up one day and started using it on his face and he has since gone on to buy his own as he not only enjoys the experience of shaving with it but also the amount of money saved on razor blades.

Safety razors require one metal blade that can last for several months before needing to be replaced and they often come packaged in a simple cardboard box with a piece of paper around each blade. They offer quite a saving compared to disposables. To recycle the used blades, I store them in a metal container under the sink and when we have filled it, I take it to the nearby specialist recycling depot where they accept metals.

Investing in a reusable electric shaver, waxer or laser hair remover are all possible waste-reducing options but most people are happy with a simple safety razor.

SHAVING GEL

We replaced this with a bar of soap which has a rich lather. My husband uses one made from natural ingredients and labelled as a specific shaving soap, but I'm happy using any soap with a rich lather.

TOOTHPASTE

Once again, personal preference and requirements will mean different solutions for everyone. As with deodorant, I simply use bicarbonate of soda to brush my teeth. I don't miss the mintiness of toothpaste and I'm too lazy to make a tooth powder or paste from scratch – often they require too many ingredients and I can't always source them all package-free. My husband, however, doesn't enjoy the experience of brushing with bicarbonate of soda so we have found a pre-made natural paste that comes in a recyclable glass jar or cardboard packaging. Excitingly there are more and more toothpaste options coming on the market, from pastes packaged in easy-to-recycle metal tubes or glass jars and dental tabs available from bulk which also contain fluoride for those who feel they need it.

TOOTHBRUSHES

The only fully compostable toothbrush currently available is one made from wood with boar hair bristles. Personally, I'm okay with this but unsurprisingly I know many friends and family members who aren't quite up for brushing their teeth with pig hair. The next best thing is a bamboo toothbrush with plastic bristles which minimizes the amount of plastic waste as the bamboo handle can be composted.

FLOSS

I bought a reusable floss container with floss refills from an online store many years ago. I simply order the refills and place them in the glass jar which has a metal lid. Alternatively, you could try repurposing a piece of silk material. Simply pull some threads loose and use them to floss.

SANITARY CARE

I chose a reusable menstrual cup (most are made from silicone but some are also made from fairtrade natural rubber) and I love it! Friends who have started using one also now swear by it. If it's not something you're willing to try or it doesn't suit your body then there are also reusable cloth pads (these are nicer than they sound), reusable tampons (I personally haven't tried them) and period pants (these can collect two or three tampons' worth of period blood and some are made from organic cotton).

TOILET PAPER

I buy a box of 48 tree-free rolls which come individually wrapped in paper. The company donates 50 per cent of their profits to water charities and I like the quality. You can also try buying from hotel supply stores as they often come loose in a large cardboard box. If you're willing to quit toilet roll altogether, washable reusable cloths or a bidet attachment are potential alternatives.

FACE WASH

I simply wash my face using the same bar of soap I use to wash my body. Honey also makes a lovely face wash. Just massage onto your face, let it sit for a few minutes, then use a damp face cloth to help remove it thoroughly. It always leaves my skin feeling super soft!

FACE MASK

I mix clay bought from bulk with a little water to make a simple face mask (see page 210).

BODY SCRUB

Try using coffee grounds, salt or sugar mixed with a little oil and get scrubbing.

MAKEUP REMOVER

Olive oil bought from bulk works perfectly. Massage the oil over your face, then remove with a warm, damp, reusable face cloth or towel. The makeup will simply melt off.

COTTON BUDS

Try buying a reusable metal ear pick instead. If you must use cotton buds, look for ones where the stick is made from card instead of plastic, which come packaged in a simple cardboard box.

TONER

Dilute one part apple cider vinegar with one part water (change the ratio to suit your skin if needed – some people dilute with as many as four parts water) and use instead of a toner. Honestly, I'm lazy and don't use toner but I hear good things about this alternative. Apply to skin after cleansing using a reusable face cloth (avoid the delicate eye area). Let it dry and follow with your moisturizer. Store the toner in a cool dark place and shake before using.

SIMPLIFY YOUR BEAUTY ROUTINE

THE LOWDOWN

Makeup is still not as waste-free as I would like it to be. I've been disappointed by DIY mascara, lip/cheek stain and face powder recipes, the majority of which ended up in an explosion of mess in the kitchen and me chipping beeswax off the surfaces for weeks afterwards. So instead, I decided to support brands who use natural ingredients and better packaging. I did have some success using cocoa powder in place of bronzer and brown eye shadow, so I have continued to use this and it's available to buy from bulk.

My foundation comes in a metal tin with a small plastic tamper seal which isn't ideal but it is a heck of a lot less plastic than most. My one lipstick also comes packaged with some plastic which is recyclable.

I have tried using natural alternatives to hair dye (such as lemon juice or chamomile tea rinses to lighten) but wasn't satisfied with the results. In the end, I decided to get highlights done professionally from a local organic hair salon where the products they use are generally kinder on my skin and the environment. When using foils, I ask the hairdresser if I can bring them home with me in my reusable cloth bag, where I rinse them thoroughly to make sure no product remains and then recycle them properly. I also request no plastic shower cap when having hair dyed all over, preferring to wait longer for the dye to develop. Usually, explaining that I'm keen to reduce waste means people understand.

TO DO

Simplify your makeup kit. I realized a mascara, eyeliner, foundation, bronzer, a lip/cheek stain and a lipstick were my essentials.

BEFORE YOU START

Consider how much makeup you need to wear. Less is often more!

Think about what you actually use on a regular basis.

simple first steps

1 **Minimize your makeup bag to your essentials.**
Use up what you can and, if you want, return unwanted items to the company explaining why you will no longer be purchasing their product (their packaging sucks!).

2 **Choose multipurpose products where possible.**
Would a tinted SPF work as both foundation and sun protection? Try a cake mascara in a metal tin as an eyeliner and eyeshadow as well.

3 **When buying new products, research options.**
Choose those that are packaged in less plastic or brands that offer refills (see the Resources section, page 214).

A NOTE ON FIRST-AID KITS

Medicines and prescriptions are often unavoidable and I would never advise putting your health at risk just to reduce your waste. Where possible, when buying over-the-counter remedies, choose cardboard or glass packaging and avoid plastic blister packs which are often mixed with foil and are difficult to recycle. Instead, look for ones made only from foil.

Return any out-of-date prescriptions and medicines to the pharmacy where they will be disposed of safely. Do not throw away in your general waste. Some items, such as used asthma inhalers, can be dropped off at a pharmacy to be recycled. See if your local pharmacy offers this service.

Plasters are often handed out without consideration. Excitingly there are now some on the market that are completely biodegradable and can be added to the compost bin. Most of the time I have found that a small piece of tissue or cloth secured in place with some brown paper tape or string will suffice when it comes to dressing small cuts.

GO THE EXTRA MILE!

- **Find a product packaged in glass, cardboard or metal.**
If something you buy comes in recyclable plastic, see if you can go one better on the material or find a refill.

- **Buy refills rather than new.**
See if the company offers a refill service for their beauty products.

- **Set up an online store selling zero-waste beauty products.**
My friend did this after struggling to source products.

- **Try taking one less shower per week.**
Use a washcloth and a little warm soapy water to freshen up and tie your hair back or wear a stylish hat if it's looking a little unwashed. This saves water and means using your products 52 fewer times a year.

- **Donate your hair to a company that makes wigs for cancer patients.**
Perfect if you have long, undyed hair and fancy getting it cut short.

- **Send products containing microbeads back to the company.**
Do not dispose of or use products that contain microbeads (small plastic particles) as they contaminate water systems and oceans. They are now banned in some parts of the world

- **Consider permanent hair removal.**
As an alternative to shaving.

WEEK 4

CLEANING & GEEKING

For those of you who know me, you may be thinking 'Kate...talking about cleaning? Really?' I'm not going to be winning any Domestic Goddess awards any time soon but since simplifying our cleaning habits and embracing a zero-waste lifestyle, I can finally muster up enough enthusiasm to keep our home looking respectable.

Secondly, I want to encourage you to remind yourself why you started on this waste-reducing journey. I've found reading up on topics around plastics, waste, health and beauty products to be a great source of motivation. This is not intended to guilt you into doing anything, but act as a reminder of why you felt passionate about making a change in the first place.

CLEANING

THE LOWDOWN

Once upon a time, the cupboards under my kitchen and bathroom sinks were crammed with coloured bottles; a spray for this and a gel for that — each containing synthetic chemicals now thought to cause serious health issues. Swapping to natural and simple cleaning products can be a bit of a challenge at first as we are used to associating the heavily fragranced smell of cleaning products with 'cleanliness'.

My husband was a big lover of cleaning products and he was always a little overenthusiastic when it came to spraying the antibacterial surface spray. So when I announced that we would be replacing his beloved cleaning products he stood for a moment in shock before saying 'I'm gonna fight you on this!'. I said if he wanted to continue using his cleaning products then he would have to make the effort to go out and buy them, which never happened! Thankfully we've both come a long way since then. As someone who has mild asthma, he now notices that his breathing worsens when around cleaning products and is more than happy wiping surfaces with our white vinegar and water spray.

TO DO

This week is about reviewing your current cleaning practices and products, and trying to find better alternatives. You will need to assemble a zero-waste cleaning kit and could consider making some of your own simple cleaning products from the ideas below.

BEFORE YOU START

- Review your laundry routine and see if you can reduce the number of loads per week.

- If you need to employ a cleaner, research one that uses natural cleaning products and support their business.

- Switch to a green energy supplier if you haven't already.

simple first steps

1 **Clean with vinegar or vodka.**
(See page 200–201) or find
an eco-friendly multipurpose
refill replacement.

2 **Try making your own products.**

3 **Air and rewear your clothing.**
Do not automatically toss it in the
laundry basket after only one wear.
Jeans can be washed less often.

4 **Dry your clothes outside.**
The sun will also help bleach whites.

5 **Label your dry cleaning.**
(See page 110).

6 **Use natural moth repellants.**
You can use bars of soap and
natural cedar balls.

7 **Iron napkins at a high
temperature to sterilize them.**

8 **Try wool dryer balls.**
Use these instead of dryer sheets
to soften laundry and make
drying more efficient.

9 **Replace fabric softener
with white vinegar.**

10 **Use reusable cloth rags.**
These are a great alternative
to disposable wipes.

Things to Remember

Before we begin zero-wasting your cleaning products, below are a few things to remember.

Ignore the Marketing

Do your best to disregard the marketing hype and commercials! You do not need to buy a separate bathtub scrub, shower spray, toilet cleaner, oven cleaner and stove cleaner. Embrace simplicity and not only will your cleaning cupboard be less cluttered, your wallet might feel a little fuller too.

Antibacterial Products

Over the years, powerful marketing campaigns have convinced us that we need their latest products to fight bacteria in our homes but in actual fact antibacterial soap is no more effective at killing germs than regular soap.[9] The term 'antibacterial' is often used to incentivize people to buy their product. Some experts believe that there may be a link between our sterilized 'antibacterial' environment and a decline in health.[10]

Health

If you need further convincing, I'd recommend using the EWG Skin Deep database (see page 217) which looks at the ingredients used in our cleaning (and beauty) products and assesses how hazardous they may be and what health issues they are linked with.[11]

It is also worth considering just how 'clean' our homes really need to be. Unless we're working in a hospital environment where extreme hygiene standards are required, it is completely unnecessary to have an absolutely spotless home and scientists now believe that the insides of our homes are more polluted with chemicals than the outsides![12] Embracing low maintenance still means our homes can be tidy, presentable and clean but we don't need to be using harsh, potentially toxic chemicals to sanitize every surface daily.

Convenience Products

Disposability in the world of cleaning products has also risen over the years, with disposable wipes becoming more and more popular. Most are made from plastic, meaning they won't biodegrade. Even if it says that it is 'flushable' on the label, these should never be flushed down the toilet as they cause enormous blockages in the sewer system as they can't break down.

THE ZERO-WASTE CLEANING KIT

When it comes to a zero-waste cleaning kit, there is no need to DIY everything, but some people like knowing exactly what is in their products and making your own can be more affordable. For others, buying a ready-made product, preferably one with eco-credentials from a refill or in simple plastic-free packaging, will be best. I choose to do a bit of both. If your local bulk store or health food shop doesn't carry cleaning products, you can find many eco-cleaning products available online, packaged in paper, card, glass or metal. These are my cleaning essentials:

WHITE VINEGAR

Use as...

- All-purpose cleaner.

- Fabric softener.

- Dishwasher rinse aid.

- Disinfectant.

- Shower cleaner.

- Rust remover.

I use white vinegar for most of the cleaning around the home – don't worry, the smell disappears after 20 minutes or so and you can add a few drops of your favourite essential oil if you want to disguise it. I am now lucky enough to have white vinegar available to me in a refill at my local bulk store but up until fairly recently I simply bought it in glass bottles from the supermarket and recycled the plastic lids. If you can only find it in plastic, buy the largest container you can afford and store.

Be careful, though. Never mix vinegar with bleach, nor vinegar with hydrogen peroxide. These combinations emit toxic vapours. Also, don't mix white vinegar with castile soap or baking soda to clean with as they will cancel out each other's cleaning properties.[13]

To make a Basic All-Purpose Cleaning Spray, follow the recipe on page 200. It can be used on kitchen worktops, sinks, floors, showers, mirrors and more! However, do not use vinegar if you have granite or marble surfaces – instead try cleaning these with Disinfecting Vodka Spray (see page 201).

As fabric softener, simply add a splash of white vinegar to your washing machine to soften clothing.

As a rinse aid in the dishwasher, add white vinegar to the rinse aid compartment.

To maintain the machine, once a month empty the dishwasher and set it going. After about 20 minutes, throw in a cup of white vinegar and close the door to complete the cycle. This tip came from a dishwasher maintenance guy whose wife was also into reducing the amount of chemical cleaning products in their home. It's also a great idea to read the manual for your machine as you may be able to set it to work with your local water hardness, making it more effective at cleaning.

As a disinfectant to clean chopping boards and surfaces, use undiluted white vinegar. Simply spray on and wipe clean.

As a shower cleaner to inhibit the growth of mould and remove soap scum, spray undiluted onto tiles in the shower. Soak the shower head in diluted vinegar to descale if limescale builds up.

To remove rust, simply spray undiluted vinegar onto the rust then scrub with a toothbrush or steel scrubber.

WASHING UP LIQUID

Use as…

- Washing up liquid.

- Surface cleaner.

- Floor cleaner.

- General cleaner.

I live in a hard-water area and no matter how many different homemade washing up liquid recipes I've tried, none of them has worked. I once tried making it from soap nuts (small brown berry shells that contain saponin – a natural cleaning agent – which can be used in place of laundry detergent) but it didn't work for me. Not only did the soap nuts fail to wash our dishes clean, but it released a putrid smell.

Liquid castile soap is a popular choice in place of washing up liquid but it really depends on how hard or soft your water is. It is widely available from bulk and works wonders for general cleaning around the home but it left a strange residue on everything. I suspect this is mostly due to the hard water in our area, so feel free to try these methods out for yourself, especially if your water is soft. I have found an eco-friendly washing up liquid refill works perfectly for me and I don't have to bother making anything!

Check out your local bulk store or health food shop to see if they have an eco-friendly cleaning product refill selection.

For cleaning surfaces, including granite and marble, use a drop of eco-friendly washing up liquid or liquid castile soap (preferably from a refill) on a damp reusable cloth and wipe. Rinse with a damp cloth if necessary.

For washing floors, add a few drops to a bucket of warm water and get mopping.

To clean most items around the home, use on a wet cloth or dilute in a bucket of warm water. It can be used for everything from cleaning toys to scrubbing muddy shoes.

BICARBONATE OF SODA

Use as...

- Scrubbing paste.

- Oven cleaner.

- Deodorizer.

- Laundry power.

I can buy bicarbonate of soda from bulk but it may also be available in paper bags or cardboard boxes.

To make a scrubbing paste, mix with a little water to form a mildly abrasive paste. Use for cleaning the bathroom or any tough, baked-on grime in the kitchen.

To make a homemade oven cleaner using bicarbonate of soda, see the recipe on page 205.

Use to deodorize the home – to freshen carpets, rugs, upholstery or mattresses – simply sprinkle with bicarbonate of soda, leave for 24 hours then vacuum.

To make a homemade laundry powder using bicarbonate of soda, see the recipe on page 203.

WASHING SODA

Use as...

• Dishwasher powder.

• Laundry powder.

Also known as soda crystals or soda ash, washing soda can be exceptionally hard to find without plastic packaging. I have only managed to find one French brand available in a cardboard box but it is expensive and I have to order it online which means it comes with extra packaging. I was delighted to discover I could make my own from bicarbonate of soda which I can easily find in bulk! You may be lucky enough to find it available to you from bulk or in a cardboard box but, if not, you'll find the instructions for making your own on page 202.

I actually only use it to make dishwasher powder as I cannot find any without plastic packaging where I live. I prefer to buy an eco-friendly laundry powder from bulk or in a large recyclable paper bag but you might like to make your own.

To make a homemade dishwasher powder using washing soda, see the recipe on page 204.

To make a DIY laundry powder using washing soda, see the recipe on page 203.

CITRIC ACID

Use as...

- Dishwasher powder.

- Toilet stain remover.

- Descaler on kettles and irons.

I buy citric acid in a simple recyclable cardboard box from a local hardware store or from bulk.

To make a homemade dishwasher powder using citric acid, see the recipe on page 204.

As a toilet stain remover, sprinkle citric acid (about 125g/4oz or several spoonfuls) into the toilet bowl and let it sit overnight. The next day, scrub with a toilet brush to remove stains. I tried various ways to keep our toilet bowl clean, including the often-recommended vinegar or bicarbonate of soda, but nothing has worked as well as citric acid.

BAR OF SOAP

Use as...

- Hand and body cleanser.

- Stain remover.

- Moth repellant.

For me, a humble bar of soap made from natural ingredients and sold in minimal (or zero!) packaging is extremely useful around the home as it cleans most things. If you prefer liquid soap, look for liquid castile soap available from bulk or try melting soap bar ends with hot water to make your own. There are even some available to buy online that are sold in glass bottles. Avoid mixing soap with vinegar as it breaks the soap down, making it ineffective.

Use for hand washing and in the shower instead of liquid hand wash and shower gel.

As a stain remover, use a bar of soap on clothing – simply wet and rub onto the stain before washing.

To repel moths and keep clothes smelling fresh, simply leave a bar in your drawers.

A NOTE ON ESSENTIAL OILS

They're not really essential when it comes to a zero-waste cleaning kit, but they can be a nice addition, especially if you want a fresh aroma in your home. I stick to a handful that work for my cleaning kit: tea tree, peppermint and rosemary are all said to hold antibacterial properties. These can be tricky to find in refills, so look for brands that use glass bottles with minimal plastic packaging. Alternatively, steep citrus peels in a jar of vinegar and, after a week, use it for cleaning. It smells lovely.

MY SIMPLE CLEANING TOOLS

Everybody's needs and standards are different when it comes to cleaning, so find cleaning tools that work for you. I've adapted and changed over the years, but below is an example of what I tend to use.

Glass or Metal Spray Bottles. These are ideal for your own all-purpose cleaning spray or refills. You could also repurpose a bottle and simply add a spray top.

Reusable Cloth Rags. Choose reusable cloths in place of disposable wipes and paper towels. Avoid cloths made from synthetic microfibres as they will shed tiny plastic fibres into our waterways when laundered. Reusable cloths made from wood pulp cellulose – a plastic-free alternative to synthetic microfibre cloths that can biodegrade at the end of their life – are another option. Any old rags or cloths made from natural materials will work.

Old Toothbrushes. These are great for scrubbing hard-to-reach areas around the taps and corners of the shower.

Toilet Brush. Choose one made from wood with natural bristles.

Steel Wool Scourer. This removes stubborn, baked-on food. Can be recycled.

Wooden Washing Up Brush. Look for natural bristles which can be composted at the end of life. Go for one regular dish brush and one bottle brush.

Squeegee. This is perfect for wiping away any residue left on glass mirrors or surfaces. Look for one made from steel and natural rubber.

Natural Rubber Gloves. These are useful for protecting hands when cleaning or doing any yucky jobs. Look for ones made from natural, FSC-certified rubber which come packaged in a simple recycled cardboard box.

Bagless Vacuum Cleaner. If you have carpet in your home, then you'll likely use one. Choose the best you can afford.

Paper Bin Bags. Either upcycle a paper bag, find tutorials online to make your own from newspaper or buy some.

We also have a cleaner visit our home twice a month to do a thorough clean but you'll be pleased to know she uses only white vinegar, bicarbonate of soda and reusable cloth rags. The company is a natural cleaning service and I like supporting their business. If you're like me and cleaning really isn't your strong point, then I'd recommend supporting a local natural cleaning service too. I also swear it's the secret to a happy marriage!

WHAT TO DO WITH OLD CLEANING PRODUCTS

We're going to look more at decluttering later in this chapter but if you're desperate to clear your home of unwanted cleaning products now that you've embraced some zero-waste alternatives, then try donating them to people who still use and want them. If you don't feel comfortable passing these on, you could return them to the company with a note as to why you will no longer be using them.

LAUNDRY TIPS

According to Fashion Revolution, 25 per cent of the carbon footprint of a garment comes from the way we care for it.[14] Simple actions – such as washing less often, air drying in the warmer months, spot cleaning, using an eco-friendly laundry powder or liquid and choosing natural fibres – all make a difference.

In the world of zero waste, some like to take it to the extreme and I have heard examples of people foraging for chestnuts (!) to use in place of laundry powder as they have a saponifying action (like soap nuts) when added to water. Personally, I'm not sure it's sustainable or realistic to expect people to source chestnuts in their local park every autumn. I also tried making my own laundry powder (see page 203), but I now favour eco brands that offer refills.

Adopting eco friendly laundry powder has meant that our clothes no longer harbour a synthetic fragrance. This is both good and bad. It has been great for my health but with the exceptionally hard water where I live, washing our clothes at 30° – which is said to be more eco-friendly – has left our laundry smelling a little stale. (According to the Energy Saving Trust, washing at 30° uses 40 per cent less energy in a year than washing at hotter temperatures[15] and, according to the Waste and Resources Action Programme (WRAP), cooler water doesn't break down fibres as quickly, which can help clothing last longer.) In the beginning, we ended up having to wash our clothes more often, each time crossing our fingers that the stale smell would disappear. After a lot of washing and testing different laundry liquids and powders, I finally discovered that by washing at a higher temperature (around 40–50°), the odour disappeared.

At first I felt a little guilty. After some thought, I decided a higher temperature was actually better for our situation and we wash our bedding and towels at a hotter temperature anyway. We had switched to a green energy company – meaning we weren't supporting the burning of fossil fuels – and we were washing our clothes a lot less frequently once we switched to a higher temperature, thus saving on resources. Simply airing items between wears meant we needed to wash them even less. If you live in a soft-water area, you may not need to wash your clothing at higher temperatures. When we stay with family in a soft-water area, we can wash our clothing at 30°.

In the extremely wet and cold months when we're forced to use the dryer instead of sitting in a condensation-filled room with clothes draped everywhere, I use 100 per cent wool dryer balls. They reduce drying time and leave laundry super soft.

A NOTE ON DRY CLEANING

Although I don't dry clean clothing very often, there are a few pieces that need sprucing up once a year, such as my winter coat or an occasion dress. Normally this means collecting garments in single-use plastic but I've found I can avoid this by taking my clothes in a reusable suit bag with a large tag saying 'no plastic please' written on the front. When collecting, the items are hung in the suit bag without any other packaging and I return the hangers to the dry cleaners to reuse. I have found a dry cleaning company that uses non-toxic dry cleaning methods and they are happy for me to bring items in a reusable suit bag.

GO THE EXTRA MILE!

Simplifying cleaning habits and products is one way to reduce waste in the home, but try the following to reduce water and energy waste too.

- **Take shorter showers to save water.**

- **Place a bucket in the shower to collect water for plants.**
  This is especially useful in the hotter months.

- **Turn off the air conditioning at night.**
  Try sleeping with a light, slightly damp sheet over you instead. This has a wonderfully cooling effect and saves energy.

- **Turn off electrical equipment at night.**
  Swtiching off wifi, TVs and phone chargers will save energy.

- **Could you install solar panels and generate your own electricity?**

- **Turn the thermostat down a few degrees in the winter.**
  Just use blankets and extra layers to stay cosy.

- **Try cleaning out your inbox.**
  Sending and receiving emails can use up energy, so the fewer unwanted emails the better. This will also save time. Unsubscribe from automatic mail outs if you don't read them.

GEEK OUT

THE LOWDOWN

By this point, especially after all that cleaning, you may need a little reminder as to why you started making all of these changes. Well, you'll be glad to hear that this next task involves putting your feet up!

I often find that when I feel a little discouraged, watching a documentary or reading a book on the topic of waste can be a surprising pick-me-up. I know, I know, they don't sound like an ideal way to pass the time but, trust me, they can be a great boost and genuinely very interesting. See the Resources section, page 214 for suggestions on my favourite films, books and blogs.

simple first steps

1 **Choose a documentary that interests you.**

Watch it with your partner, family or housemates if they're keen. Start with a topic you feel most passionate about. Is it plastic waste? The fashion industry? Minimalism? The bottled water industry?

2 **Make a visit to your local library.**

See if it has any of the books mentioned in the Resources section (see page 214) to borrow, or find a second-hand copy online. If buying new, support your local bookshop and remember your reusable cloth bag!

GO THE EXTRA MILE!

- **Host a screening.**
You could do this in your community and show
a documentary that you found to be impactful.

- **If you're part of a reading group, suggest one
of the titles that address waste.**

- **Start a campaign or petition to implement
more waste-saving services.**
This could be in your area or it could be a way to highlight bad
practices. See if you can involve local press and politicians.

- **Volunteer at a charity working to fight wasteful systems.**
If you can't donate time, then consider setting up
a regular monthly payment instead.

WEEK

DECLUTTER!

Now that we've introduced new habits and embraced reusable or plastic-free alternatives, it's time to let go of clutter. This may take some time, which is why this is the only task set this week. I encourage you to at least make a start and dedicate some time to letting go of items that no longer serve you. Trust me, your future self will thank you!

DECLUTTERING

THE LOWDOWN

I've found decluttering to be an ongoing process but, over the years, the amount gets less and less as the few items that now come into our home have been carefully thought out and built to last. Although I love decluttering, my organizational skills are still a work in progress. I'm no minimalist and actually enjoy some stuff, but I do find myself feeling lighter, less stressed and generally happier the less clutter I have. I also believe most people have more than is needed; do we really need a TV in every room? How many items of clothing in our closet do we actually wear? And don't get me started on that junk drawer!

While some things can spark joy and remind us of happy memories, hoarding things 'just in case' can sometimes be a symptom of a deeper problem – whether it's the loss of a family member, a traumatic experience, feeling lonely or even depression. Too many things not only create visual clutter, they can also increase our stress levels by consuming our time and energy in cleaning or storing them.

It may feel counterintuitive to be getting rid of things, especially when this whole book talks about reducing waste. But that's exactly the point of decluttering. We're freeing up those items that are sitting unloved and unused at the backs of our cupboards or in the garage, to be enjoyed and put to use by other people who genuinely need them. We help to boost the second-hand market, which means people may be more likely to look for the item they need at their second-hand store or at an online site selling pre-loved items first, before automatically buying new.

It can also open our eyes to the sheer amount of stuff we didn't know we had stored away. This can be useful moving forward, as we may realize we no longer need to buy more things, as something similar is probably already available at home.

TO DO

Different decluttering methods work best for different people. Whether you go room-by-room (kitchen, bathroom, then bedroom perhaps), or category by category (books, clothing, toys, kitchenwares, cleaning products) is up to you. I like to tackle one room at a time, but you should start with a category or room that seems fairly achievable. Remember, choose the easy wins first and the rest will feel less overwhelming.

BEFORE YOU START

Question everything! When you are decluttering, take
a single item at a time and ask yourself:

Do I use or need this?

Could I sell it?

Could I donate it?

Can it be repaired and if so will I use it?

Do I keep it out of guilt?

Is it a duplicate?

Could I access a digital version or store it in an online cloud system?

Could I rent it instead?

simple first steps

1 **Place items into separate piles labelled 'keep', 'not sure', 'donate', 'sell', 'recycle' and 'trash'.**
Try not to spend too long having a sentimental moment with every item you touch. Start with the easy things you're keen to let go and start to enjoy the feeling of less. Remember, these things are a waste if not in use, so releasing them to be enjoyed by others really is the most sustainable option.

2 **Try collecting sentimental momentos in one box.**
Do we really need stuff to trigger memories? Sometimes we only need one item to remind us of a significant moment. Store photographs online or arrange in a beautiful photo album.

3 **Organize the rest!**
Once you have decided what to keep, set about storing these items in an orderly manner. Give everything a 'home', a place where it lives when not in use and remember to return it to the same place. Not only will this save time hunting through random drawers, it also means your home will look tidy and feel calmer. And you won't be tempted to buy what you can't find.

KEEP

Make an effort only to keep what you truly love. When it comes to clothing, try it on and be honest with yourself as to whether or not it flatters you, still fits, or makes you feel good. Avoid falling into the just-in-case trap. Too often we keep things for those rare 'what if' scenarios which will likely never happen. Consider how many times you've actually used or worn something in the last few years.

NOT SURE

There will inevitably be pieces you come across when clearing out that aren't an obvious 'keep' or 'go'. For these items, give them a little time. I find asking for a second opinion from my husband or impartial friends often helps make an informed decision. Otherwise I store these items away in a suitcase for a few months and see if I miss or need them. If not, then it's time to let them go.

SELL

Selling items you no longer need helps keep them at their highest value and means they will be loved for longer by someone else.

For good-quality clothing, take them to a local dress agency (aka consignment store) where, if they sell, you keep a percentage of the sale price. Using a consignment store also means the items are more likely to stay local, reducing packaging and shipping. Online versions offer a similar service and resale apps are widely available.

When listing items to sell online, take decent photos and highlight any signs of wear and tear. The more honest you are, the happier the buyer will be.

For random artifacts or anything that is too difficult to sell online, consider holding a carboot/garage sale. This can be a fun day and great way to involve the children. Just resist browsing the other stalls, no matter how tempting they may be.

DONATE

When something is a little too worn to sell, or perhaps there is little demand, then donate it. Charity shops are a good place to start as they accept a wide variety of things and the money generally goes towards a good cause.

If you have large furniture or bulky items, ask if the charity shop will collect from you or contact your council to see if they can collect things to be recycled. There may be a small fee attached for this service, but it will be worth it!

Offering items to friends and family is another option, especially if they have shown an interest in something you're giving away. But don't burden them with items they don't really need.

RECYCLE

Anything that can be recycled, should be. You'd be surprised by what can be recycled, including CDs, phones, small electricals and even light bulbs.

Most items will need to be taken to a specialist recycling facility or store where they can be collected. Do a little research whenever you come across something you would usually toss in the bin. Could it be recycled?

TRASH

Inevitably there will be some things that cannot be kept, sold, donated or recycled. Accept that this is the case and use them as a reminder to buy better in the future. Try to consider the end life of every item purchased from now. Where possible and, if you feel ready, return the item to the manufacturer with a letter explaining why (I'll address this in more detail in Week 6, see page 132–42).

MOVING FORWARD

So you've decluttered, sold, donated, recycled and re-organized your stuff. What a task! But it will all have been for nothing if you continue your purchasing habits. Moving forward, take some simple but effective actions to limit the amount of things you bring into your home.

• Quit buying stuff for the sake of shopping. Often we browse the high street or online stores out of boredom. Try doing something else instead: baking, dining out with friends, learning a new skill.

• Avoid making impulse purchases. Wait a while and seriously consider if you really need to buy something. Look into borrowing or renting instead, or simply doing without.

• Limit exposure to adverts. I know this sounds impossible but the fewer magazines you read, the less likely you will want to buy new things. Why should you waste your hard-earned money on products that will clutter your home and likely come with toxic side effects?

• Learn to look after your things. When possible, get them repaired or altered. Keep them clean and follow the care instructions. Not only does this keep them in use for longer, it also means we support craftsmen and repair services, keeping their skills in business.

• Join the sharing economy. Most things are available to rent or borrow, whether it's a car, a bike, tools, cameras, tech, clothing, baby stuff, toys, camping equipment, a holiday home, costumes or books. Ask friends and family or look online for services that specialize in renting items.

• If something is truly needed... Buy second-hand or new from a company whose ethics you want to support. Buying things we need isn't bad – the mindless consumption of things we don't need is.

GO THE EXTRA MILE!

Decluttering can be an ongoing process, but over time I find there is less to deal with. If you're already pretty organized, then try some of the following:

• Take on a no-spend challenge.
Set yourself a weekly or monthly budget for permitted purchases such as groceries, bills and any essentials for school/work/life, but limit the non-essentials

• Go through the items that you have packed away.
If you have items sitting in storage or at your parents' house, deal with them now.

• Declutter your social media accounts.
Only follow ones you really enjoy and that inspire you.

• Enjoy a digital detox.
Take a break from your phone, computer and TV for a weekend.

• Declutter your computer and any external drives.
This means you won't have to buy more storage later on.

WEEK

START COMPOSTING & DO SOMETHING!

This week is all about embracing the magic of composting and being an active citizen. You may have already started composting, especially if you're lucky enough to have a collection service available or a large garden. But for those of you who have either put it off or are limited in your options, then now is the time to start thinking about ways to embrace composting.

START COMPOSTING

THE LOWDOWN

It took me a little while before I started composting and my only regret is that I didn't start sooner. I chose a scandi-style wormery for our small city apartment which looks stylish (you wouldn't guess it was even a worm bin at first glance) and can be used both inside and outside, depending on available space. This might sound a little strange, but I ordered a bag of composting worms online and they arrived a few days later in an envelope with some soil. All I had to do was place them in their new home with some dampened shreds of paper or cardboard, a little extra soil and a few food scraps to get them adjusted. Within a few weeks they were able to accept most of our food waste (except things such as meat, dairy and citrus peels).

Composting food is nature's way of recycling waste and it can make a dramatic difference to the amount of waste we end up throwing out. As the contents of your compost grows, you'll start to notice just how little you have to throw away (especially if you've followed all the steps).

TO DO

The best advice I can give to anyone about composting is to just start. You'll figure it out as you go and there is an abundance of information and troubleshooting available online if needed.

BEFORE YOU START

Do some research to find out what is available to you in your area. I will discuss some of the possible options on the following pages.

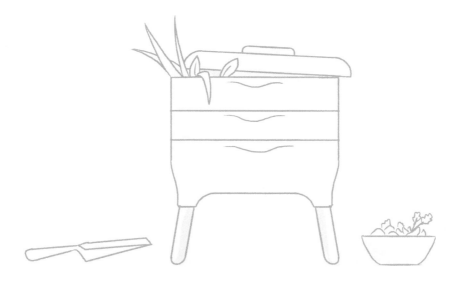

simple first steps

1 Use your composting system.

Start making good use of it as soon as possible.

2 Be careful to respect the system.

If using a worm bin, keep an eye on the contents. Check for mould, moisture or any food the worms don't like. If composting in the garden, read up about what can be composted successfully.

3 Educate others!

Let partners/family members/housemates know what can and cannot go in the compost bin. Make a handy guide or list to keep close by if needed.

KERBSIDE COLLECTION

This is the simplest solution, especially for city dwellers, so if you have it available to you, start using it now. You may need a specific compost caddy from your council so check with them first. Each location will have different rules about what they can and cannot accept, so familiarize yourself with your local compost collection guidelines. They often accept meat, dairy and bones, which are tricky to compost in a home composting system or worm bin. If your local authority doesn't offer this service, see if there is a private compost collection service to which you could subscribe.

COMPOSTING DROP OFF

Some places have dedicated locations, such as farmers' markets, where people can bring their compostable waste to drop off. I love this idea as, most of the time, the compost goes straight back to the farmers. If your neighbourhood has a composting drop off location but you can only visit a few times in the month, try freezing your food scraps to stop them rotting and attracting pests. Keep them in a container in the freezer then simply take the container with you or place the frozen food waste into a compostable paper bag.

WORMERY

If you don't have a compost collection or drop off location nearby, the next best option in my opinion is using a worm bin. There are now lots of different styles to suit your aesthetic (some are even designed to look like furniture). You can either buy one from your local gardening centre, online or, if you enjoy making things yourself, it can be fairly easy to make your own by stacking repurposed plastic trays with some holes drilled in (see the Resources section, page 214, for details of a tutorial).

In the beginning, try to notice which foods your worms tends to avoid (they usually look like they're trying to escape from whatever it is you've added recently) and keep an even balance of greens (vegetable and fruit scraps, loose tea leaves and coffee grounds, washed and crushed egg shells) and browns (newspaper, brown paper, card, hair, nail clippings, fabric scraps). I like to place any new food waste into one corner and see if they like it.

In the end, simply add the compost to your pot plants, garden soil or donate to a friend of family member. You could even give it away for free online.

BOKASHI BIN

This system relies on a special bran-like powder packed with beneficial bacteria which ferment food scraps, creating a sort of pre-compost. The upside of bokashi composting is that it can also break down meat and dairy products.

You need to buy bags of bokashi bran regularly as each addition of food waste requires a handful of bran to be added. The goal is to let as little oxygen in as possible, so pack the food waste down tightly each time. Every other day, the leachate (which is a by-product of the anaerobic composting system) needs to be drained so make sure your bokashi bin has a tap to remove the liquid. After tightly sealing and leaving the food waste to ferment for about two weeks, the contents – while recognizable – will have become a sort of 'pre-compost'. This can be buried in the garden to finish breaking down or added to your worm bin.

This works best alongside a worm bin as it can pre-digest meat and dairy as well as speed up the process of breaking food down. Using it as a stand-alone system didn't work for me, especially with limited outdoor space and nowhere to bury the scraps once fermented. It is also worth

noting the smell. When working correctly, the smell will be yeasty and slightly sour but if working badly, it is eye watering.

ELECTRIC COMPOSTER

Sadly, there don't seem to be many of these on the market but if you're considering one, it's worth noting that they cost a little extra money to run (electricity) and usually need filters which have to be changed. The units themselves can also be a bit of an investment. On the plus side, they can process everything within a short time frame (ranging from a few hours to a few days), including cooked and uncooked meats, dairy and citrus fruits.

OUTDOOR COMPOST

If you have a large garden then this is a good option. Simply choose a spot and start adding green and brown matter to a pile. If you want, you can enclose the compost pile in an old bin or container with a lid and with the base removed. Or buy a compost bin. If your compost bin has a base, then you'll need to add composting worms to get things moving.

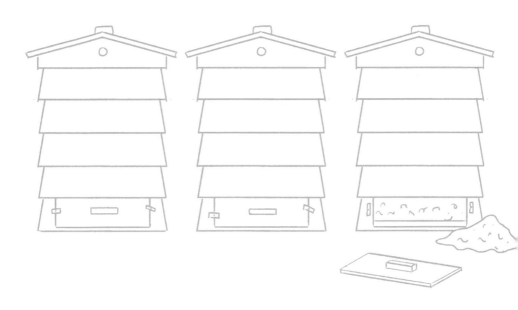

GO THE EXTRA MILE!

If you're already hooked on composting or feel you have no other options available to you, then there is still more you can do.

• Set up a pet waste composter.
If you have the outside space and a pet such as a dog or a rabbit, consider setting up a specific pet waste composter – but do not use the compost on edible plants and do not compost cat waste (see page 216).

• Ask the local authority to run a food waste collection service.
Even if this involves sending them an email once a month.

• Could you set up a residential food waste collection service?
If none currently exists in your area, this could be a good solution.

• If you own a restaurant or business, set up a food waste bin.
Arrange for it to be collected to be composted. There are lots of services like this available to businesses.

DO SOMETHING!

THE LOWDOWN

Taking action is one of the best ways to combat feelings of frustration which usually crop up at some point during a zero-waste lifestyle. Whether it's picking up trash, hosting a talk or writing to a company, there are some great ways to influence positive change.

TO DO

Be creative and think of ways you could make changes outside of your home. Not only does this help the wider community, it could also renew your motivation and make you feel your efforts really are worthwhile.

BEFORE YOU START

Consider joining a local zero-waste group. They often host events, talks and general meet-ups and it can be a great way to find like-minded folks. It can also be a good source of support and morale.

simple first steps

1 Write a letter.

Choose a company whose packaging you have ended up with and believe could be improved. Enclose the packaging for added emphasis.

2 Pick up some litter.

Either on your own, with friends or as part of an organized group. Clean and recycle as much of it as possible.

3 Use your skills to share what you have learned so far.

Write an article for a local publication, give a talk, watch a documentary you found moving with friends or host a screening. Whatever you fancy, do it!

AM I A FAILURE?

So you've embraced reusables, started shopping loose and decluttered your home. But despite all of these positive, life-changing actions, it's hard to ignore that waste, especially plastic, is everywhere! Once you start to notice it, you can't 'unsee' it.

A walk is accompanied by plastic water bottles on the kerbside, plastic bags in the trees and packaging floating in the river. On a short flight, I am stunned by the amount of single-use disposables being handed out. A trolley heaving with a leaning tower of throw-away plastic cups, plastic water bottles, plastic-lined coffee cups with plastic lids, plastic stirrers, plastic-wrapped sandwiches, plastic-covered chocolate bars and snacks rolls past me and, moments later, two large plastic bin bags are ready and waiting to collect all of the items that were so carefully stacked on the cart only moments ago. Rest assured, I am fully aware of my carbon impact when flying overseas. But add to that the amount of oil, water, carbon and waste in the form of single-use freebies, over-packaged consumables and disposables...am I the only one seeing this?

This is an inevitable part of the zero-waste lifestyle. Thoughts such as 'why do I bother when there is so much waste in the world?' may creep in from time to time. Feelings of failure will rise up, especially when you can't avoid buying something packaged, or a straw ends up in your drink despite requesting 'no straw please'. These feelings are totally normal and will pass with time. I like to remind myself of all the positive changes I have made in my own little world and think of how much waste I used to contribute towards the problem compared to today.

You may also start to notice that conversations with friends and family members may be a little awkward to navigate. It's not easy finding the balance of being interested in your friend's new top or shoes, while your internal monologue goes something like: 'Your top is made from polyester, a plastic, which won't biodegrade and has likely forced the underpaid maker of that garment be exposed to harmful, toxic chemicals which will not only be detrimental to their health but also pollute their local waterways and environment...and don't get me started on the microfibres that thing releases when you do your laundry!' But resist ranting at people. It only makes them feel under attack. Instead, lead by example. Wearing sustainable and organic brands or second-hand items yourself may invite compliments such as 'I love your top, where's it from?'. If someone shows an interest in your lifestyle, then by all means elaborate. But don't lecture!

It can also be all too easy to slip down a path of perfectionism, which leads to serious frustration, and that can lead to the dark side...which we all know is best avoided! Focus on the positive and, where possible, remind yourself that you are doing your best at that moment in time. Perfection is overrated.

Respond! How to Write a Letter

Inevitably, no matter how diligent we are about reusing and reducing the amount of packaging in our lives, some will magically find a way of appearing. Perhaps an online order comes wrapped in plastic or a reusable item designed to reduce waste comes packaged in a non-recyclable box. Whatever it is, firstly remember it's not your fault. I have spent far too long feeling guilty over pieces of plastic that came into my home until I remembered all of the other amazing habits I had created. And actually this small offending item was most likely out of my control.

One of the most empowering things I have found in response to a piece of unwanted packaging is to use it as a reason to contact the company and suggest an alternative. Often, I enclose the packaging along with the letter for added emphasis and ask them to dispose of it 'responsibly'. The lady at my local post office always asks for safety reasons what is in my parcel and I think now she could guess what my response will be: packaging.

Customer feedback can be extremely powerful. A friend of mine once told me about an industry insider who said that for every piece of feedback a company receives, the company imagine the 10,000 other people who think the same thing but haven't bothered to write and let them know. And with the rise of social media making it extremely easy to contact a company with your feedback, taking a few moments to send them a message can result in them making a change.

Some might argue that returning packaging is a waste of further resources (envelopes, paper, fuel) but I truly believe these simple actions are worth the potential larger impact. For example, as a result of customers returning non-recyclable crisp packets to a well-known manufacturer, they have now announced they will be changing their packaging to a recyclable alternative within a year. On a personal note, I have seen local stores stock reusables and encourage refills as a direct result of my feedback and even a laundry powder brand remove the plastic scoop that came with each purchase.

When writing a letter to a company, try to keep it short and sweet. I like to take the 'sandwich approach' and remember to keep the tone of any communication respectful and polite.

Top layer. Start with a compliment, such as why I love their brand or products.

Filling. Why I am writing and the issue with their packaging.

Bottom layer. Suggest alternative solutions and, if possible, give examples of similar brands doing things better (nothing like a little competition to incentivize change!). Highlight how the change could benefit them, such as saving their company money or improving their customer loyalty and brand image.

I tend to stay away from going into environmental details. This often comes across as quite 'heavy'. Instead, I briefly mention that as a customer I am unable to dispose of the item in a 'responsible' way and would like to see change from their company. I also never leave my contact details as I've learned that I usually get a template response consisting mostly of excuses as to why they package something a certain way and it merely adds to more waste coming into my home.

If the idea of writing a letter sounds like too much of a chore then use emails or company contact forms instead. It shouldn't take longer than 10 minutes to hop online and write a simple message, following the 'sandwich' layout just mentioned. If possible, attach a picture of the packaging, samples or item for emphasis.

Finally, there's always social media. While I generally limit my time online, I do find it useful when contacting a company as many now have dedicated teams ready and waiting to deal with customer feedback via social media. It can also be a great way of engaging others if the message is publicly visible with retweets or replies from other like-minded people showing the company that you are not the only one concerned with their packaging choices or wasteful practices. But remember, be polite. The more you rant and rave, the less seriously they'll take your feedback.

Top layer: start with a compliment (such as why I love their brand or products) ↘

Dear Washing Powder Company,

I have been a big fan of your product for many years. I love that you use natural ingredients and I have been very impressed with the results.

Filling: why I am writing, and the issue with their packaging →

While I appreciate the product needs to be protected, I wondered if you had considered a plastic-free packaging alternative which could be easily recycled as I notice your current packaging is labelled as 'not recyclable'. I also wanted to highlight that the plastic scoop that comes in each packet may not be necessary for most customers.

Bottom layer: ↗ finish by suggesting alternative solutions and if possible give examples of similar brands doing things better

I have seen similar brands to yours package their products in a simple paper bag or sturdy cardboard box, which can be easily recycled in my kerbside collection and would like to suggest that you consider doing the same. Regarding the scoop, I notice that they simply suggest quantities in spoonfuls, meaning customers can use a spoon they already own. Removing the plastic scoop could save your company money as well as reducing the amount of plastic waste.

In the meantime, I enclose the non-recyclable packaging and plastic scoop for you to dispose of responsibly.

Warmest,

Kate

LITTER
PICKING

I used to find the idea of joining a large organized beach clean up a little overwhelming. Perhaps it's my introvert personality, but I much prefer to pick up trash whenever the moment grabs me. From the moment I step outside my home, I see litter so, when I can, I pick it up and dispose of it in a more responsible way. If I can add it to my recycling, then I will, otherwise I feel it is better to place it safely in a bin than watch a bird try to eat it in the street.

Whenever we visit the coast, I almost always end up picking up trash that has been washed up on the beach. There's something about it being so close to the water and the potential for it soon to be lapped up by a wave that makes me want to pick it up even more. I usually use a gardening glove and several reusable cloth bags and simply fill them with whatever I can collect. Again, if I can clean up some of the plastics and recycle them at home, then I will. Otherwise I simply add them to the bin. If possible, I like to save a few items to return to the brand (if I can tell which brand the litter was made by) with a letter explaining where I found it.

PUTTING ON A TALK

Despite working as a TV presenter for over 10 years, I still get nervous when it comes to talking to a live audience. But, I've found, the more passionate I am about a topic, the easier it is to stand up and share. If you're happy putting together a few slides and enjoy sharing your experiences and tips for reducing waste with others, then why not consider doing a talk at work or in your community?

Share funny stories and keep it personal to make the lifestyle far more relatable and your audience will come away feeling inspired instead of guilted into making change. If you have pictures to demonstrate some of the reusables you have found useful, or how you go grocery shopping without packaging, then add them to your presentation.

Try to focus on the positive – no one likes to sit there and be told they're killing the planet and all of its inhabitants everytime they use a takeaway coffee cup. Perhaps they have simply never considered it before or thought to question why they accepted it as normal.

Keep it straightforward – it's basically a version of show and tell. I use the pictures on the slides to prompt my talking points and I share funny anecdotes along the way. I like to highlight small, achievable changes I've made over the years while keeping it relatable. I sometimes start with a trailer from the documentary *A Plastic Ocean*. The images of people and animals struggling to cope through the mountains of plastic waste are quite shocking but it's short enough to give a brief impression of the problem. The rest is focused on positive changes I've made.

Head to YouTube to find other zero-waste talks and notice what you enjoy about them. Do you like the energy of the person talking? How about the pictures they're sharing? Do they give examples of practising zero waste in everyday life? Consider why you find them engaging. It can be tempting to fact-dump on people to make yourself feel more like an 'expert' but I've found the fewer stats, the more interested people are. Use one or two if needed for emphasis, but generally all they do is leave people feeling guilty.

If standing up in front of people and doing a talk isn't your vibe, then why not organize a brunch, coffee morning, workshop, drinks evening or panel discussion instead? There are so many ways to share your new insights with friends, family and community. You may even find a local network of zero-waste enthusiasts already in your area.

GO THE EXTRA MILE!

If you want to get real serious about an issue...

• Start a campaign to address a specific type of waste.
This could be something that is prevalent in your area (you could even create a specific hashtag on social media). Is your local park littered with plastic drinks cups in the summer? Contact local news outlets and politicians to tell them about your idea and start a movement.

• Make a piece of art from waste materials.
This could be a sculpture, or anything made from repurposed items.

• Start your own local zero-waste group.
You can share your knowledge and gather support.

• Get your workplace involved.
Why not talk to your manager or HR about hosting a litter collection at lunch, screening a documentary, replacing disposable cups with reusables, putting on a talk or even trial composting food waste.

ZERO WASTE
IN ACTION

Now that we've introduced some new habits in our everyday lives, we can start applying them to different scenarios. The following examples are some of the ways in which I have managed to reduce waste. Remember, every event or scenario will be different so go with the flow and try to use it as a learning experience. Find the fun in thinking creatively!

THE ZERO-WASTE WARDROBE

How many times have we found ourselves exclaiming 'I have nothing to wear!', despite research telling us that in many countries, people don't wear even half of the clothing they own? What a waste! Not to mention the polluting ways in which those clothes were made or the unethical working conditions for the garment makers.

The thing is, I like clothes – but since adopting a more sustainable closet, I love them even more. I love the stories behind each garment. I love discovering who made them and how they were lovingly crafted. I adore the high-quality, natural fabrics. Even caring for my clothing has magically worked its way up my priority list.

In my opinion, fashion should feel as good as it looks. And don't worry, a more sustainable closet doesn't mean you have to conform to a certain style or aesthetic. It's totally up to you. When it comes to a zero-waste wardrobe, there are several things to consider.

BUY LESS!

The world now consumes about 80 billion new pieces of clothing every year, which is four times more than we consumed just two decades ago.[16] Not so long ago, we had four seasons of fashion. Now we have 52, with new clothing appearing on the high street every week thanks to fast-fashion brands. Most of it is made from cheap synthetic materials and not designed to last. Buying less is one of the best ways to fight our unsustainable fast-fashion habits. See if you can limit your clothes shopping to only once or twice a season. And buy only what you really need and have carefully considered.

Capsule wardrobes – where people limit themselves to a set number of versatile and wearable items of clothing, shoes and accessories per season – are becoming popular. The idea is to try to focus on what you already own, instead of bringing in new pieces each season. Find the right balance of clothing for you as long as you're wearing the items regularly.

CHOOSE WELL

Thinking carefully and choosing wisely when it comes to clothing means we often end up with cherished pieces which work for our lifestyles and we will love for longer. No more impulse purchases!

Start by searching for items second-hand. Not only is this more affordable, it also saves on resources and gives a pre-loved piece a new lease of life by diverting it from landfill or recycling.

- If charity shops aren't your vibe, try dress agencies or consignment stores. They offer a more upmarket selection of pre-owned designer goodies at around half the original price.

- If buying an item second-hand online, remember to request no plastic packaging from the seller.

- Have an item altered if the fit isn't quite right. This can also be done for items you already own but you rarely wear.

- Sizes can be misleading and vary between brands, so always venture outside of your usual size and try something on to see how it fits.

THINGS TO CONSIDER

• **Durability.** Look for items that are well made and designed to last. Some brands even offer a repair service or a lifetime warranty. Think about how many wears you will get from the item. If it's expensive, you could consider the cost per wear – the bare minimum should be 30 wears, but try to aim for 100 or more.

• **Style.** Trends fade but style lasts. With this in mind, look for pieces that will still be stylish for years to come – breton tops, classic T-shirts and good jeans are useful staples. Stick to your personal style – you'll be more likely to wear the item more often and for years to come.

• **Practicality.** Choose pieces that fit your lifestyle. What we each need in our wardrobes will differ from person to person depending on our personal style and what we do – outdoor adventurer, office worker, landscape gardener, artist...

• **Versatility.** Select pieces that can be worn more than one way or can be carried through the seasons.

• **Sustainability.** If you're unable to find something second-hand, buy new from a brand that uses sustainable materials and ethical practices. There are now lots of truly beautiful sustainable brands that are not only using better materials but also offer repairs services (see the Resources section, page 214).

• **Lifespan.** Renting outfits or borrowing a special dress for an event is a great idea. Ask friends or family, or search online for clothing rentals.

MATERIALS CHECKLIST

- **Avoid synthetics.** This includes polyester, acrylic and nylon which are made using petroleum. They pollute our environment at every stage, from production all the way to disposal. Research has shown that synthetic clothing sheds microfibres in the washing machine which slip through the filters and make up a significant proportion of ocean plastic.

- **Choose natural fibres.** Fabrics such as cotton, wool, hemp, silk and linen are more likely to be compostable. Tencel is a manmade fibre made from plant cellulose and is also compostable.

- **If buying cotton, choose recycled or organic cotton.** The majority of cotton is made from genetically modified seed which requires a huge amount of pesticides and water. Organic cotton, on the other hand, maintains soil health and biodiversity, is largely rain fed, and gives farmers food security and independence. The more we buy it, the more farmers will convert to growing cotton organically.

- **Look for certifications.** This includes GOTS (Global Organic Textile Standard) which is considered to be the gold standard when it comes to organic certification. FairTrade focuses on improving the working and living conditions of smallholder farmers but also never uses genetically modified cotton. Cradle to Cradle certifications assesses materials and products against five quality categories – material health, material reutilization, renewable energy and carbon management, water stewardship and social fairness.

- **When buying leather, look for vegetable-tanned leather.** The chemicals used in conventionally tanned leather mean it cannot biodegrade.

- **Recycled cotton, wool and silk are a good option.** However, recycled synthetic materials such as polyester will release microfibres into the water system.

RULE 3

MAKE IT LAST

According to a study by Fashion Revolution, a non-government organization campaigning for fair working conditions in the fashion industry, 90 per cent of our clothing is thrown away long before it needs to be, thanks to our culture of 'fast fashion' and outdated laundry habits.[17] Extending the life of each item of clothing by just three months would result in a 5–10 per cent reduction in each of the carbon, water and waste footprints,[18] so caring for our clothing is super important.

• Follow the care instructions on the label but bear in mind that most delicates don't need to be dry cleaned and can simply be put on a wool wash in the machine or washed by hand.

• Wash clothing less often as this helps it last longer. Spot clean between wears if necessary. If you can, wash at a cooler temperature as this maintains the fibres for longer. Fibres such as wool need washing far less often and jeans should only be laundered once a month according to denim experts.[19]

• Repairing is caring, so invest in pieces that come with repair built in. Check to see if aftercare is something that is offered by a brand when buying new. Shoes are often easy to have repaired. If you don't have the sewing skills, support a local alterations service instead. Even things such as moth holes can be repaired by an expert.

END OF LIFE

Inevitably, we all have to get rid of clothing once it's worn out or no longer suits our lifestyle, but never throw any away!

- **Reselling.** If in good enough condition, try reselling either online or via a consignment store/dress agency. Otherwise clothing can be donated to a charity shop.

- **Repurposing.** If the garment is really past its function, try repurposing it. Could you use the fabric to make reusable cloth bags (you can never have too many!) or cleaning rags?

- **Recycling.** Take any worn out items to a clothing recycling bin to that it can be shredded and turned into car seat stuffing or insulation.

- **Composting.** Compost threads and pieces of natural fabric too tiny for recycling.

ZERO WASTE AT WORK

I'm lucky in that I work from home but as our flat is incredibly small, keeping things minimal is key. I've realized that we don't need a home printer as we rarely need to print anything and the cost of ink is crazy expensive. Instead, I use the local library or printing service if necessary.

I donated most of our pens as I found we simply weren't using them and, instead, bought a convertor for an old fountain pen. There are many beautiful second-hand ones available online, some with built-in pistons or convertors which means no need for a disposable cartridge – you simply fill up from a glass jar of ink. I even found some ink made from natural oak gall, but any ink will do nicely.

First, minimize what you truly need – often we have office supplies sitting around, just in case. Then look for reusable, recyclable or compostable alternatives to the things you do need.

A ZERO-WASTE STATIONERY KIT

- **Pen.** Find one fitted with an ink convertor, or purchase a convertor for a pen you already own.

- **Pot of ink.** Choose one packaged in glass.

- **Pencil.** Choose a refillable lead holder (although the lead refills are usually packaged in plastic), newspaper pencils or a regular wooden pencil without an eraser on the end.

- **Natural rubber eraser.**

- **Binder.** Made from recycled cardboard and metal hoops, or a durable all-metal ring binder. Look for recycled card tab inserts.

- **Paper tape.** Use as a replacement to plastic sticky tape. It can be easily recycled or composted.

- **Stapler.** A metal paper clip, or cutting and folding the corners of the paper work just as well – or invest in a stapleless stapler.

- **Coloured pencil.** Use this instead of a highlighter.

- **Planner.** Use an online planner or buy an easy-to-recycle one made from recycled content. You could also make your own from reused paper.

WASTE AT WORK

I have met several people over the years who have become increasingly frustrated by the wasteful practices that go on in their offices. Many have taken it upon themselves to suggest introducing reusable cups, trialing a composting system or simply recycling paper waste. If you are able to present a waste-saving idea as an opportunity to save the business some money, as well as being better for the environment, then your company will likely take more notice. I once visited a well-known company that offered reusable takeaway coffee cups for their staff to grab on their way out for a coffee run. Such a great idea and so simple!

Organizing talks can be a great way of inspiring staff. I once visited a firm of lawyers as I was asked to do an informal presentation over lunch about some of the simple swaps I had made personally to reduce my waste. I was pleasantly surprised by the number of people who turned up and even more surprised by the amount of questions I was asked at the end. People were clearly keen to start making changes.

If your workplace is a little resistant to change and shows no interest in reducing their waste, then try to stay positive and focus on your own actions. Leading by example often inspires others to take action. So bring in your reusable coffee cup and casually mention how you get a discount for using it at the coffee shop across the road. It won't be long before you spot colleagues bringing their own. Other things you could do include:

Bringing in your own lunch.

Keep a set of reusable cutlery. Use a container at work to grab lunch to go.

Save compostables and recyclables. Bring them home with you and deal with them appropriately.

WAYS TO REDUCE YOUR OFFICE WASTE

Reuse envelopes. Save packing materials to reuse if you need to post items. Save the shredded paper to use instead of bubble wrap.

Try printing on both sides of the paper. Adjust the margins to maximize space used. Where possible, go paperless. This also means that if you need to access a document while away from home, you can do so via an online cloud storage system.

Choose paper and stationery made from recycled content. This can be recycled easily at the end of its life or, even better, reused by someone else.

Refuse business cards. Take a photo if needed, which you're less likely to lose, and consider whether you or your employees really need one.

Avoid laminating!

Compost shredded paper. Or recycle it if it's accepted by your local recycling.

Compost pencil shavings.

Purchase second-hand office supplies. Or you can rent larger items such as printers and copiers.

Repair equipment when it breaks. Laptops and computers can often be repaired or returned to the manufacturer to be recycled if completely beyond repair.

Find a green office supplies retailer. See what plastic-free or reusable alternatives they have available.

Email documents and invoices. Do not print them.

Save scrap paper. Use this instead of notebooks or sticky notes.

Choose lickable stamps. The stick-on ones come with a plastic-lined backing, making them difficult to recycle.

Avoid gifting freebies. This includes company pens, keychains and diaries. If you must give something, then a company-branded reusable cloth bag would not only be useful to most people but likely serve as free advertising.

EATING OUT WITHOUT WASTE

The zero-waste lifestyle generally encourages more cooking from scratch, which is not only healthier but cooking can be a therapeutic process.

I'm a real foodie and LOVE going out to eat! Shopping is voting, and the same goes for where I choose to eat. I like to support restaurants and cafés that use sustainable practices, have organic and local ingredients on their menu and offer reusables. There are even restaurants who make great efforts to reduce their waste. Here are some of the ways I reduce waste when eating out:

1 Refuse

Say 'no thanks' to paper napkins, straws (even if they are made from paper – do you really need it?), plastic cocktail stirrers and condiment sachets. Most tables in a restaurant are already laid out when you sit down so simply return the paper napkin to the waiter and say 'I'm not going to need this, you can reuse it'. Or I sneak it back onto the pile!

2 Bring Your Own

Bring a reusable napkin. If you suspect there may be some leftovers at the end of the meal, bring a container with you to take them home. My husband even has his own reusable toothpick. When going to the cinema, bring your own snacks (from bulk) or your own bag of popcorn (see page 195).

3 Bring it Home

If the restaurant doesn't compost, then bring anything that can be composted home with you. I do the same with recyclables if possible.

4 Give Feedback

If the restaurant you visited could do something a little better, get in touch and let them know! Give positive feedback as to why you love their food, ambience, service, then offer some useful suggestions that could replace any wasteful practices you noticed.

TAKEAWAY

We still enjoy the occasional takeaway. I try to favour cardboard, foil or paper if packaging is necessary. For example, if ordering a pizza to be delivered, I choose one that comes in nothing but a simple cardboard box (no plastic pizza stand!).

I've found taking a reusable container into a takeaway and asking them to put the food straight in works well. Some food-delivery apps allow customers to opt out of plastic cutlery. If in doubt, email or call the establishment and ask them what packaging they use.

FAMILY & FRIENDS

One of the most common questions from people starting a zero-waste lifestyle is, 'How do I get my husband/wife/girlfriend/boyfriend/housemates/family to stop making so much waste?' I'll admit, when I started out, there may have been one or two explosions of frustration at my husband when he brought home something that was wrapped

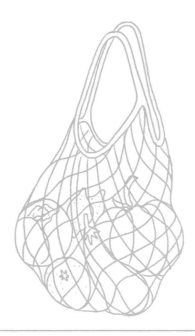

in single-use plastic, or another receipt that would get left on the side (receipts often contain plastic so they can't be recycled). He's now fully on board with the zero-waste lifestyle and often talks about it more than I do with friends and family. But this transformation was a slow process (for us both) so be patient.

I quickly learned that guilting anyone into doing something doesn't last. Micromanaging doesn't either. All I could do was take care of my own actions and involve my husband as much as possible. In our household, I do the grocery shopping so the purchasing power is mostly mine.

WAYS TO GET LOVED ONES INVOLVED

Focus on our own actions and lead by example. It's far more powerful than simply telling someone what they should do. Bring them with you when you're buying groceries or let your partner try your reusable razor if they're curious!

Find out what drives them. Is it saving money, improving health or learning new skills? Mention how your zero-waste lifestyle helps with that.

Watch a documentary together. One that highlights issues, such as those about plastic waste.

Be encouraging and grateful. Praise them for any changes that they are willing to make.

Offer to do the hard work for them. They might want to find a zero-waste alternative but don't know where to look. Mention that you saw an alternative and, if they want to try it, you'll pick it up for them next time.

VISITING FRIENDS & FAMILY

When I am a guest in someone else's home, I do my best to play by
their rules. Where possible, I will always seek to use reusables instead
of disposables without forcing my ideas on anyone. If someone has
questions, I'm more than happy to answer. Be respectful. If I'm offered
a cup of tea from a tea bag that I know contains plastic, I first consider if
I actually want a cup of tea. If so, I accept graciously. Alternatively, I could
ask if they have any ground coffee instead, but the main point I want to
make here is that I'm not super strict with myself at other people's homes.
It can also be useful to step outside the world of zero waste for a moment
and remind yourself how most people live. It is easy to forget what is
'normal' and it's a lovely reminder of just how far you've come.

EVENTS &
CELEBRATIONS

Hosting events can be a wonderful way of showcasing just
how beautiful and uncompromising a zero-waste lifestyle can be.
If people like your style, they'll ask questions but will likely not
even notice you've done anything different.

PARTY FOOD & DRINK

Try to find options sold loose from bulk such as olives, cheeses and cured meats. Cookies and cakes can usually be bought without packaging from bakeries or delis – simply take a container or reusable cloth bag with you. If you enjoy baking, try making them from scratch using ingredients found loose or packaged simply in paper. You could also make your own dips such as hummus to serve with sliced vegetables. Homemade popcorn makes a quick and easy alternative to crisps (see page 195).

Infuse jugs of tap water with herbs or slices of fruit. This will make them a little more special. If you don't want to make your own soft drinks, look for cordials and sodas in glass bottles. If you have a sparkling water maker, use this to add a little fizz to your drinks or turn tap water into sparkling.

Serve wine and beer bought from a refill. If you don't have these options near you, look at the packaging and choose the one with the least plastic. Corks from wine bottles can be sent off to be recycled and glass bottles can be recycled time and again. Beer bottle caps usually have a layer of plastic on the inside which makes them impossible to recycle but they can be saved and turned into Christmas tree decorations or given away for free online. Otherwise, choose drinks in aluminium cans which have an extremely high recycling rate and will likely be back on the shelf as a can within 60 days! Avoid the plastic six-pack rings that often hold beer cans together. These can be lethal to sea creatures if they end up in the ocean.

If guests want to bring a bottle, relax! Do your best to recycle it.

Compost or donate any leftover food. If possible, ask guests to bring a reusable container in case they want to take some home instead of a goody bag!

PARTY TIPS

- **Give people notice about your waste-free ways.** Do this before they rock up to your door with a bag of party poppers and 50 balloons! A simple email explanation can be effective.

- **Replace disposables with reusables.** Choose real cutlery and glasses (opt for metal if you're nervous about breaking glass) and reusable cloth napkins.

- **Question if something is really needed.** Straws, balloons and goodie bags are very wasteful.

- **Keep it simple.** From decor to food and themes.

- **Consider the packaging.** Sometimes packaging can't be avoided so choose options that can be easily recycled or composted. For example, when choosing an Easter egg, go for one that comes in a simple cardboard shell.

- **Candles are a great way to help set the mood.** Choose ones made from natural wax, such as beeswax, instead of paraffin candles which are made from petroleum. At the end of their life, melt the final pieces into an empty egg carton and use as a firelighter, or simply compost the remaining natural wax.

- **If you're the guest, don't complain about the disposables used.** If possible, ask if you can pinch a reusable plate or glass from their cupboard (remember, wash, dry and return it afterwards) or simply bring a reusable napkin with you and use that to hold food. Bring your own cup for drinks if you think it may be necessary.

- **Avoid giving or accepting goodie bags!**

CHRISTMAS

Christmas can be the trashiest time of the year with household waste increasing by 25–30 per cent during the festive period in the US, Australia and the UK.[20] Not so long ago, I remember feeling the stress of the Christmas build-up as I marched down the high street trying to find a gift for every member of the family. But it doesn't have to be that way. Since embracing a zero-waste lifestyle, Christmas has become about spending quality time with my loved ones, eating good food, enjoying walks and giving a few, well-thought-out gifts – often experiences, vouchers or something that is truly needed.

Live trees. A few years ago, we bought a potted tree from a local company. It lives on our balcony and I simply bring it inside for Christmas. You could also rent a tree if outside space is limited. The tree can continue to grow, sequestering CO_2 and not ending up in landfill.

Cut trees. Nearly 100 million Christmas trees are sold in Europe and North America each year[21] and they can take years to decompose in landfill, so make sure you recycle it – check your local authority website.

Alternative trees. Consider decorating a large foraged branch, making a reusable wooden tree from reclaimed wood or simply decorating a house plant.

Fake trees. If your heart is set on a fake tree, buy second-hand and vow to reuse it for the rest of your Christmases to come. This means you aren't creating a demand for new plastic.

Fairy lights. Finding eco-friendly fairy lights is a challenge. I use the lights I've had for the past five years and will keep using them until they expire. They are plug-in LED lights which use a fraction of the energy of regular fairy lights and they don't overheat.

GIFT WRAP

Wrapping paper is used once, then discarded. It is often difficult to recycle due to the mix of materials.[22] Some alternative ideas are:

The from-behind-the-back reveal. Oooooooh! It's cute and completely waste free. Ta-dah!

Reusable gift wrap. Use a piece of decorative cloth or try a reusable cloth bag as gift wrap – two gifts in one!

Newspapers or magazines make good gift wrap. Just make sure you choose the headline carefully. My mum wrapped my Christmas gift in newspaper once and the headline read: 'Christmas with the family? I'd rather have £250'. Thanks Mum!

Swap plastic sticky tape for twine. Or brown paper tape which can be recycled or composted.

DECORATIONS

Avoid adding more plastic baubles to the collection each year. Consider dried orange slices hung with thread, cinnamon stick bundles with repurposed ribbon or twine, pinecones or salt dough stars (despite my creative attempts they still look like a four-year-old has made them!). There are also plenty of second-hand decorations available, or try supporting skilled makers by purchasing hand-crafted decorations in natural materials.

Use biodegradable glitter. Regular glitter is made up of tiny pieces of plastic. Natural foliage, such as a sprig or two of holly, some mistletoe and dried eucalyptus, can add a wonderful festive touch. Look for a reusable advent calendar – there are lots of different ones to choose from, made from wood or material.

CARDS & THANK YOU NOTES

Use recycled cards. If you can't resist sending a card, choose one made from 100 per cent recycled content, which is easily recyclable (no glitter, foil or foam bits) and sold without plastic wrapping.

Send electronic cards. It is a handy, low-waste alternative.

Assess the people on your Christmas card list. If you're still sending a card to someone you met on holiday once, perhaps you don't need to continue.

Reinvent your thank you notes. Could you call the gift-giver or send them an email instead?

WEDDING CHECKLIST

When I got married in 2014, I was still fairly new to the world of zero waste, but I did what I could. I have never been in to big white weddings, so we enjoyed a small ceremony with close friends and family, followed by a large party with friends at a nearby restaurant. We loved it! But whatever style of wedding you choose, there are always ways to reduce the number of bin bags.

Send e-invites. Instead of physical ones. If real invites are preferred, choose those made from recycled content and make sure they can be recycled or composted. Some even come with seeds embedded in the paper, which can be planted when the invite is buried in the soil.

Set up an experience gift list. There are many online sites that allow guests to contribute towards activities on your honeymoon.

Hire decorations. This might be tableware, chairs, tables, linen, flowers and the groom's attire. Some venues come ready decorated and may only require a cleaning fee for napkins and table cloths.

Try renting or finding a second-hand dress. I had a very specific design in mind and, after months looking, I decided to ask a friend who had just graduated from fashion school to make my dress. Focus on natural materials and buy just the right amount of material. If designing your own, consider if the style could also be worn for future events.

Let the venue know you are keen to reduce waste. Let them know that you want reusables in place of disposables. See if they can compost or donate any leftover food and refrain from offering disposables.

Choose natural confetti. Dried flower petals are available to buy, or make your own. You could also use a hole punch to make confetti from fallen leaves.

TRAVEL

We generally take one or two short-haul flights each year, and one long-haul flight every couple of years. However, travelling – especially by plane – can be filled with an epic amount of waste. From the moment we arrive at the airport, we're bombarded with stickers, tags, duty free, disposable water bottles, coffee cups and food shrink wrapped to within an inch of its life. And that's before we've even boarded the plane. Once seated, we spend our time unwrapping a synthetic blanket from its single-use plastic packaging, eating and drinking from disposable plastic containers with plastic forks and knives (which all get discarded only moments later) and flicking through the list of chemical-laden products on offer in the in-flight magazine.

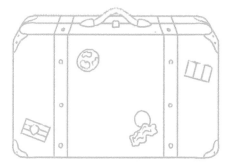

Due to strict regulations around food-contaminated waste, the majority of waste on a flight ends up being burnt or buried. Even recyclables are quarantined or incinerated due to fears of contamination from overseas diseases or pests and most airports do not offer recycling facilities. It's not just typical waste that gets tossed. As well as used cutlery, newspapers and food and beverage packaging, airlines often throw away blankets and headphones!

As well as all the physical waste, air travel can also be a huge source of air pollution, not to mention all of the environmental issues associated with tourism. But I believe that travel can be good for us — exploring the world and deepening our connection with nature can be a strong reminder as to why we want to tread a little lighter.

With a little planning, preparation and simply refusing, it's possible to avoid many of the disposables that come with travel. It can be easy to think our small actions don't matter, especially since the in-flight meal gets wasted if we refuse it. But if enough people refuse the meal or request an 'opt-out' option when booking, then they may start to listen. Every disposable we refuse lessens the demand for another to replace it. Following up with a simple message on social media or emailing the airline about their use of single-use plastic is a great way to communicate your message.

PACKING CHECKLIST

When I do travel, I pack light, taking only a carry-on bag to avoid adding unnecessary weight to the plane. When I need to check a bag, my husband and I share one to minimize space. Planning ahead can really help when it comes to packing. How often do we end up bringing things we don't wear or use? Try to pack light and clever by choosing versatile clothing and only one book instead of three! Most hotels will have hairdryers and travel adapters available to use. And remember to pack the items that will help you reduce waste on your travels.

REUSABLES

Water bottle and coffee cup. Simply ask the flight attendant to pour drinks into your container. Personally, I've never been refused on a flight but I've heard from others that it can be a bit hit and miss. If you are refused, don't take it personally but make sure you follow up with an email to the airline asking them to encourage reusables and how it not only saves on waste but could also save them money!

Headphones. No need to unwrap the ones provided by the airline and the sound quality of yours will likely be far superior!

A wrap or large scarf. I use this instead of the plastic-wrapped synthetic blanket provided by the airline.

Reusable cutlery. I prefer to bring a metal spoon, but there are bamboo cutlery sets available or sporks.

Eye mask. Useful for catching some sleep on the flight.

Handkerchief. For any sniffles or wiping hands

FOOD & DRINK

Refuse in-flight food. Instead prep some of your own for your travels. Taking food through security is fine, as long as there are no liquids.

Snacks. Take dry snacks (chopped vegetables, popcorn, sandwiches and cookies are all good). Try to eat it all on the flight as taking foods into a different country can cause issues.

Water filter/sterilizer. If travelling to a part of the world where you're advised to avoid drinking the local tap water, consider investing in a reusable water-filtering device to make water safe without resorting to plastic-bottled water. Alternatively, find out before you leave if your hotel or a nearby restaurant has access to filtered water to refill your bottle. If bottled water is the only option, try to find glass bottles.

BEAUTY & PERSONAL CARE

Pack the essentials. Choose multipurpose items and share products if travelling with others. Save and reuse a clear plastic zip-lock bag. You'll need this if taking any liquids such as beauty products through security. They often hand them out, so if you don't have one, take it and save it to reuse each time you travel.

Solid beauty products. These are ideal if you're only packing a carry-on as they don't contain liquids or pastes. Solid shampoo and soap bars, deodorant sticks in cardboard tubes, tooth-tabs instead of paste are all possible options.

Liquids. Decant products into smaller, travel-size containers you've saved.

Sunscreen. Hawaii recently passed a bill banning the sale of sunscreens containing chemicals (oxybenzone and octinoxate) known to be harmful to coral reefs and sea life. Personally, I try to take a safe and sensible approach, wearing a hat and sunglasses and sticking to the shade in sunny places. When I do need sunscreen, I like to find one with minimal, natural ingredients, which uses only non-nano zinc oxide as the sunscreen in plastic-free packaging. There are now several available in compostable cardboard tubes or metal tins and if you're lucky enough to have a sunscreen refill option near you, use it.

IN TRANSIT...

Refill your water bottle. Once you've been through security, refill your bottle at a water fountain or ask the staff in a restaurant so you're ready for the flight.

Eat a large pre-flight meal. This will help you to avoid being hungry on the flight – the food will taste better anyway!

Avoid wrapping your suitcase in plastic. While it might make a baggage handler think twice before inspecting your luggage it won't stop security from opening your bag if needed.

Use an e-ticket. Avoid printing one out.

Take your recyclables with you. If you've used a disposable and it isn't contaminated with food then take it with you and recycle at your location.

Refuse! Say 'no thanks' to packaged foods, drinks, duty free and disposable hand wipes.

Decline the housekeeping in hotels.
Do this as much as possible and
participate in the towel-reuse programme.

Avoid plastic-packaged items. These will
be lurking in the mini-bar and bathroom.
Bring your own plastic-free personal
care products and refuse the single-use,
plastic-wrapped slippers.

Switch lights off. And the air-con while
you're at it!

Choose reusables. This includes glasses,
cups and cutlery at breakfast.

Take reusables on trips out. When out
and about, take a reusable cloth bag and
water bottle, and recycle where possible.

Support eco hotels. Choosing a hotel
that makes an effort to improve the
environment means you're voting with
your money.

**Rent a tent or invest in a durable one
made to last.** Do not leave it behind! Try
glamping where everything is already set
up, or invest in sturdy reusables if you go
camping often.

**Look for farmers' markets, delis and
specialist stores.** Food is more likely to
be sold loose in these locations. Research
local bulk stores on the internet before
travelling.

Check out the local recycling. Follow food
waste guidelines and do the best you can.

Choose local food and drink. This will
boost the local economy and avoid food
imports to suit our foreign palates.

Avoid postcards and souvenirs.
These just add more clutter to your
home (or someone else's). Instead, take
photos to remember your trip and send
some via WhatsApp or email to family
and friends.

Communicate. Don't be afraid to ask
nicely. In Milan a few years ago, my
husband and I arrived late and found
only one place open for lunch and it
only served food in disposables. It was
located in a food court so I asked if we
could use the reusable plates and cutlery
from the restaurant opposite. The server
loved that we were trying to reduce plastic
and ran over to fetch the reusables for us.

YOUR CARBON FOOTPRINT

As well as reducing waste when travelling, it's important to consider how frequently we travel and the type of transportation. Research has found that travelling from London to Paris by train rather than flying could cut CO_2 emissions by 90 per cent. I recently calculated my carbon footprint and flying two round trips to Europe each year kept me well within my carbon quota, while one visit to the US sent me soaring above! It is possible to pay a voluntary carbon tax when flying. Although an imperfect solution, it at least shows policy makers that we care, are conscious of our actions and may think twice before flying unnecessarily. No one is perfect – get out there and see the world, just try to tread a little lighter where possible.

Whilst it can be important to consider our carbon footprint, I do not believe it to be the only measure of our impact and it does not consider the full picture. Instead, try to focus on the positive effect that your zero-waste and eco-friendly changes will have on the wider world. For example, if you have to fly, bring your own reusables and try taking just a carry-on bag. No carbon calculator will factor in the amount of disposables you've avoided using during a flight or the power of an email to the airline suggesting that they offer a no-meal option, but you'll know that you've had a positive impact all the same. However, if you are keen to learn more about your carbon footprint, then check out the Resources section, page 214.

BABIES & KIDS

When it comes to children, I must admit I am not an expert. As I write this I am currently pregnant with my first child so my experience is extremely limited but here's what I've discovered in my research. Having spoken with various friends who have taken actions to simplify their children's lifestyles and reduce the associated waste, I have learned of some potential areas where I can take action.

First things first, keep things simple. There are now so many things that are marketed as essentials to new parents that it's easy to forget that our grandparents and parents survived perfectly well without them. Often, we are told we need a product to help our children sleep well, or another to improve their development. Consider what is truly needed and then, if something feels like it is missing, look into purchasing it, preferably second-hand!

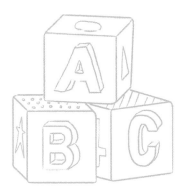

Throughout pregnancy I have been fortunate enough to receive clothing from family members who were happy to pass them on. I also found a few second-hand pieces on eBay as well as some non-maternity garments I knew I would continue to enjoy wearing for years to come but also fit my current changing shape. When you think about it, maternity wear doesn't need to mean a whole new wardrobe of clothing – choose a few simple and versatile basics such as jeans, T-shirts and larger knitwear to combine with items you already own. I must admit to purchasing some new maternity knickers (made from organic cotton) and I have no regrets!

I have bought several books (second-hand) on what to expect during and after pregnancy and one thing that keeps appearing is advice to buy disposable knickers. Having spoken to mummy friends about this, they have reassured me that some thick reusable sanitary pads and period pants will do the same job. My midwife (who seems to be surprisingly knowledgeable about reusables) also recommends reusable cloth labia pads for postpartum. I'll let you Google these, but essentially they help ensure your underwear doesn't get ruined by any sudden flows.

Throughout pregnancy I have done my best to reduce waste where possible, and even insisted on reusing the urine sample pot given to me by my midwives (they actually loved the idea). But there have been times when my waste-free ways have been less of a priority. During my extreme nausea phase in the first trimester, all I could envisage eating was beef-flavoured crisps. I called my husband and asked him to go to the nearest store and buy as many packets as he could. Let's just say he didn't recognize his wife for a few days as I sat on the sofa munching on plastic-packaged snacks! Considering this was the first time I'd eaten them in five years, I was okay with it.

NAPPIES

Around eight million disposable nappies are thrown away each day in the UK alone.[23] Often we simply think about the waste they create once used, but it's also worth considering the amount of resources that have gone into making and transporting them, as well the materials they are made from (which are usually synthetics, containing harmful chemicals and gels). Should these really be sitting in close contact with our children's skin? In landfill, disposable nappies can take hundreds of years to degrade and release harmful greenhouse gases.

Disposable nappies also cost the taxpayer money. For every £1 spent on disposables, it costs the British taxpayer 10p to dispose of them, which is why many local authorities have introduced cash or voucher incentive schemes to encourage people to use reusable nappies.

BIODEGRADABLE NAPPIES

Recently, 'biodegradable' or 'compostable' nappies have sprung onto the market and, while the intentions are good, we currently do not have a system to deal with them. Either they are sent to landfill – where they cannot biodegrade due to the lack of oxygen, light and water – or

they risk contaminating council compost collections where they won't be accepted. Please don't compost them at home as a garden compost will generally not get hot enough to kill the pathogens that may be lurking in the faeces. Some places (especially some states in the USA) have businesses who operate a compostable nappy service, which is a fantastic idea if reusables really aren't your vibe. Search online and see if you can find one nearby.

REUSABLE NAPPIES

The only arguments I have come across against reusable cloth nappies are the extra amounts of laundry required and the cost. I have spoken with friends who are reusable nappy advocates and they say that the amount of laundry tends to increase with babies anyway as they seem to attract all kinds of dirt, so adding a few extra washable nappies to the load doesn't really make much of a difference. When looking into the costs of reusables, they found that overall they actually saved money, even when accounting for increased electricity bills.

Using an eco-friendly detergent, sourcing electricity from a renewable energy source, and line-drying as much as possible can all help to reduce the environmental impact of reusable nappies even further.

Several friends have advised that investing in a few different reusable styles to see which suits you and your child best is the way to go. Nappy libraries or workshops are a good way of learning more about the different reusables. Be careful if choosing second-hand as the elastics may have overstretched, meaning they are more likely to leak. In this case, I'm personally happy to buy new and support a business making a product I'd like to see more people use, especially if they use more eco-friendly materials such as hemp and organic cotton.

You may be lucky enough to have a nappy laundering service available to you in your area. In this case, they collect the dirty cloth nappies to be cleaned and drop off a freshly washed set. Bear in mind that the harshness of products used by these services might not be to your usual eco-standard. If you can find one that uses eco-friendly cleaning products, even better. Also, check that they deliver them in disposable plastic.

DISPOSABLE WIPES

Disposable wipes, while not exclusive to babies (disposable kitchen wipes are also common), are used a lot to wipe sticky hands, bottoms and spills. When a friend took me litter picking on a paddle board on the Thames, we were shocked by the number of disposable wipes we saw. Many are made from plastic and, no matter what the packaging says, they should not be flushed. Instead, try switching to washable cloth wipes. It can be as simple as using them with plain warm water, or you can make your own solution.

TOYS

I often wonder if children really need many toys in the early stages. They seem most content with cuddles and naps (and an empty box!) but as their curiosity develops, a selection of well-chosen toys can be essential. Don't forget that you will also be given toys as gifts too.

Where possible, choose second-hand items. Do your best to stay on top of the quantity, especially if the toy no longer serves your child or they have outgrown it.

Try donating one toy for every new addition. Look for ones made from natural materials such as wood, metal and cloth. Avoid plastics, which not only break more easily but often contain harmful chemicals.

Avoid toys that only perform a few actions. Or those modelled on specific movie characters which limit imaginative play. Instead choose simpler pieces that invite creativity and stimulate the imagination, such as building blocks, art materials, dressing-up clothes, musical instruments, board games, balls and sports equipment.

Toy libraries are a good option. They allow parents to borrow toys and take part in the sharing economy. If there isn't one nearby, you could try starting your own.

Minimize exposure to advertising. This will reduce the urge for more and more new toys.

Encourage time spent together. This could be playing games, reading, drawing, making, singing and exploring outside – there's nothing quite like a freshly made mud pie!

Buy thoughtful gifts. Try incorporating experiences instead of just giving stuff. Ever since he was a young boy, my husband has been treated to an annual theatre trip by his godfather. My husband looked forward to these every year and enjoyed the time spent together – the memories have far-outlasted any toy.

Teach children to refuse, reuse and recycle from an early age. It will then become second-nature for them. Kids are great at absorbing information and they love learning. I was recently amazed to see my seven-year-old niece picking up trash from the beach on holiday after we'd spoken about how a lot of plastic ends up in the ocean. Involve them in your habit changes, explain simply why they are important and make it the new normal.

PETS

While there are various steps you can take to minimize their waste, a zero-waste pet is practically impossible. Don't be disheartened, as with the rest of the zero-waste lifestyle, it isn't about purrrrrfection (*sorry*) – just do what feels comfortable for your situation and prioritize your health and that of your pet. I am obviously not a vet or animal dietitian – please do your own research and consult a professional when in doubt.

I grew up with a house rabbit and thinking back now, I realize he was a rather low-waste pet. He wasn't fond of rabbit food pellets and spent most of his life nibbling on vegetable scraps, nuts, seeds, porridge oats, apple cores and hay. As all rabbits do, he even ate his own droppings (it helps with their digestion) and relieved himself in a tray filled with newspaper and straw. I have since read that rabbit droppings can be easily composted. Either throw them directly onto flower beds or add them to your compost pile. But avoid putting them on edible plants.

PET FOOD

Depending on what your pet needs to eat, consider some of the following options:

Buy loose from bulk. Make sure you're happy with the quality. Don't sacrifice the health of your pet for the sake of packaging.

Buy in bulk. Preferably in a large paper bag if possible.

Make the food yourself. Use real ingredients.

Choose recyclable packaging.

Ask the butcher for bones for your dog. Remember to bring a reusable tin.

Ask the company to reduce their plastic. If you buy from a small independent pet food company, ask if it's possible to reduce plastic packaging or send in a container to be filled up.

PET WASTE

This is probably the trickiest part when it comes to pets. Essentially we need industrial pet waste composting services to become more commonplace. Check to see if your town is composting pet waste. Rabbit bedding can be composted at home, as long as it is made from compostable materials such as paper, straw or wood shavings. Pet fur and nail clippings can also be composted in your regular compost bin.

DOGS

Check your local authority's advice regarding flushing dog poo down the toilet. In some places it is advised as being the most eco-friendly option, but others strongly advise against it. In remote parts of the countryside where pet waste bins are few and far between, the advice is to stick and flick your dog's poo into the undergrowth. This reduces the plastic waste, provides nutrients for the plants and is more hygienic as it is off the public pathway.

Most eco-friendly dog poo bags are either regular plastic with enzymes which eventually break it down into smaller plastic particles, or they are made from compostable plant-based materials. However, most end up in landfill where they cannot break down due to the lack of oxygen and light, or they are incinerated. Instead, try using a piece of paper from the recycling bin and place in the appropriate pet waste bin when out and about, or add to your general waste at home. There is a dog poop-scoop available made from cardboard if you're keen to reduce plastic waste (see the Resources section, page 214).

If you have space in your garden, try composting dog poo. This must be done in a separate receptacle to your regular compost and the final product should only be used as manure on non-edible plants. Cut the bottom off an old plastic bucket (with a lid) and drill holes along the sides. Do not drill holes in the lid. Dig a deep hole in the garden and sink the bucket into it. It should be covered up to the lid. Place a layer of shredded newspaper, fallen leaves or straw in the bucket, then start layering in your dog's poo. Cover with the lid and, once full, let the contents sit for as long as possible (around two years is best) until it breaks down to look like crumbly compost. Mix the contents every couple of weeks. I repeat, do not use the end results on edible plants and make sure that it is inaccessible to children.

CATS

Composting cat litter is not enough to kill the diseases associated with cat faeces, so avoid doing it. Do not flush cat litter and faeces down the toilet as they may contain a parasite called toxoplasmosis which cannot be destroyed by sewage treatment. It is lethal to marine mammals and otters if it makes its way into the ocean. Purchase cat litter in paper bags or cardboard containers or use natural materials such as sawdust to minimize plastic waste sent to landfill.

GROOMING AND FLEAS

Cats and rabbits tend to clean themselves, and castile soap bought from bulk can be used to wash your dog. Or look online for a dog-specific shampoo bar.

Flea treatments are sometimes necessary but, as with most things, prevention is key.

Vacuum the home. At least once a week.

Wash pet bedding. Do this in hot, soapy water regularly.

Frequently use a fine-toothed flea comb. Check your pet for pests.

Use caution when using essential oils to fight fleas. Some may be suitable for dogs but cats should not be exposed to any.

Ask your vet if it's suitable to feed garlic to your dog to repel fleas. Depending on the size and breed alongside any medications, garlic may be right for them.

Optimize their health and immunity. Like other parasites, fleas target less-healthy hosts, as well as puppies and kittens with undeveloped immune systems.

Consider a chemical-free metal tag. This uses a magnetic field to repel fleas and lasts up to four years.

PET TOYS & ACCESSORIES

- **Choose natural materials.** These can be composted.

- **Reduce the amount of toys to your pet's favourites.** If they have a talent for shredding soft toys to pieces within minutes, choose something more durable.

- **Reuse what you already own.** An old tennis ball, a piece of rope as a tug toy, toilet roll tubes for hamsters, rabbits and cats.

- **Choose second-hand pet toys where possible.**

- **Prioritize durability when buying accessories for your pet.** This is essential when it comes to leads, beds and bowls.

USEFUL
RECIPES

Making things from scratch usually results in reducing waste and allows you to use up ingredients and leftovers. But making everything from scratch isn't always convenient or sustainable. For a while I tried making my own bread, yogurt and tomato passata every week but I found the processes took too long and it wasn't practical. The same goes for DIY laundry powder and various beauty products. While I try to reduce all packaging, with some things I have accepted that buying a product packaged in glass, metal or card is more realistic and I'm happy supporting brands that are making an effort to avoid plastic.

Some of these recipes will help to reduce food waste, others reduce packaging waste, others I had trouble sourcing from bulk. This list is by no means exhaustive and there are links in the Resources section on page 214 for more recipes.

Each person will probably settle on a few recipes they enjoy making, especially if they are cost effective and less wasteful. But don't feel you have to make everything from scratch. Find your balance.

IN THE KITCHEN

All or most ingredients mentioned here should be available from bulk or in plastic-free packaging. Prevention is better than cure, so let's start with a few simple tricks to reduce food waste in the first place.

Buy little and often. Food is less likely to go off.

Serve smaller portions. Go back for seconds if needed.

Use your freezer to save leftovers. It will stop foods such as bread going stale, and you can keep vegetable off-cuts for making stock.

Plan ahead. Make a shopping list and stick to it. Having a rough meal plan for the week also helps minimize waste.

Ask if you're unsure when it comes to quantities. Your butcher or deli counter server can advise on how much you need per person.

Buy unpackaged. You will only buy what you need.

Included are recipes for the things I make regularly. Most have helped me to reduce packaging waste or they are so simple that buying the packaged alternative seemed ridiculous.

STOCK

I make stock once a week after working our way through a roast chicken and use it for soups or adding extra flavour to other recipes. It's delicious as a warming drink too. This is the perfect recipe for using up vegetable ends and peelings, as well as meat bones. I tend to be relaxed with the quantities, but below is a rough guide.

Ingredients

1kg (2lb 4oz) vegetable scraps

1 chicken carcass or a few meat bones (optional)

1 tablespoon apple cider vinegar (optional)

1 teaspoon peppercorns

salt to taste

Method

Place the vegetable scraps and meat bones (if using) in a large stock pot and cover with water, almost to the top. Add the apple cider vinegar if using meat bones to draw out the minerals. Add the peppercorns and salt. Bring to the boil, cover and simmer for 1–2 hours for veggie stock, 4–6 hours for chicken stock or 8–12 hours for beef or lamb, topping up the water level if it gets too low.

While still hot, strain the liquid through a sieve into a large jug, then pour into clean jars. Screw a lid onto each and leave to cool before storing in the fridge. Use within a week or freeze smaller portions.

BREAD PUDDING

I make breadcrumbs with any stale ends, but when the bread pile gets a little too high, I like to make bread pudding (and serve with lots of custard – see overleaf!).

Ingredients

150g (5½oz) stale bread, broken into chunks

75g (2½oz) raisins (optional)

4 eggs

500ml (18fl oz) milk

70g (2½oz) sugar, or to taste

3 tablespoons melted butter, plus extra for greasing

1 teaspoon ground cinnamon

1 teaspoon vanilla extract

a pinch of salt

Method

Preheat the oven to 180°C (350°F), Gas Mark 4 and grease the base of an oven dish with butter. Arrange the bread in the dish in a single layer and sprinkle with the raisins, if using. Whisk together the remaining ingredients, then pour the mixture over the bread. Bake for 45 minutes–1 hour until thoroughly cooked. When a knife comes out clean, the pud is ready. Serve with homemade custard!

CUSTARD

Instead of buying custard in a can or plastic-lined carton, I found it was incredibly easy to make my own. Save the egg white and add to scrambled eggs, quiche or bread pudding. I buy my vanilla extract in a glass jar with a metal lid, but you can make your own by placing two vanilla pods, sliced in half lengthways, in a small bottle. Cover with brandy, seal and leave for three days before using.

Ingredients

1 teaspoon cornflour
  or arrowroot powder
300ml (½ pint) milk
1 egg yolk
1 tablespoon sugar,
  or to taste
a few drops of vanilla
  extract

Method

Whisk the cornflour or arrowroot with the milk, then stir in the egg yolk, sugar and vanilla.

Pour the mixture into a saucepan and place over a low-medium heat, stirring continuously. Keep heating gently and stirring until thickened, but do not allow to boil.

PANCAKES

Pancakes are a great way to turn last night's dinner into an exciting meal. I like to make both American-style pancakes (see note below) and crêpe-style pancakes, which can be both savoury and sweet. They're so easy to make, there's really no need to buy a pre-made pancake mix, especially as many come packaged in plastic. Ideal for breakfasts, evening meals or as a sweet treat. Take this recipe as a starting point and go wild with your leftovers.

Ingredients

1 large egg
100g (3½ oz) plain flour
250ml (9fl oz) whole milk
a little butter or oil for
  cooking

Method

Crack the egg into a mixing bowl and whisk with a fork. Add the flour and milk and mix until a smooth batter forms. Heat a little butter or oil in a frying pan over a medium heat and use a cup or ladle to pour in enough batter to make a pancake. Swirl the batter around to cover the base of the pan in a thin, even layer. When little bubbles begin to appear on the surface of the pancake (after a couple of minutes), flip and cook for a further minute or two until golden on both sides. If you don't use all of the batter, simply store in a glass jar in the fridge and use within a few days.

For American-style pancakes: Simply use self-raising flour instead of the plain flour or add 2 teaspoons of baking powder. You could also add 1 tablespoon of sugar to the mixture if you like a sweet pancake (I prefer to add sweetness with my toppings).

PASTA

For the first three years of my zero-waste lifestyle, I couldn't find pasta available from bulk and all packaged pasta came in non-recyclable plastic. So I made it instead. I now have plenty of pasta options available at my local bulk store, but wanted to include it in case you find yourself in a similar situation.

Ingredients

600g (1lb 5oz) type-00 flour or pasta flour
6 large eggs

Method

Place the flour in a large bowl and create a well in the centre. Crack in the eggs and beat with a fork until the flour and eggs combine to make a smooth mixture. Pull the dough together using your hands until combined. Knead on a lightly floured surface until the dough starts to feel smooth and silky (around 10 minutes).

Most people rest the dough in the fridge for half an hour, but honestly I usually go straight ahead, split the dough into manageable pieces and roll out on a floured surface until fairly thin. I then gently roll it up and, using a sharp knife, slice into tagliatelle-style strips. Cook in a pan of boiling water for a few minutes until tender, then serve.

RUSTIC CRACKERS

*I found crackers difficult to source without plastic packaging. Initially,
I was more than happy to enjoy cheese on a slice of toast or with some apple.
But, when we visited a friend's house, I decided to make some crackers to
take with me. They went down a treat and tasted delicious!*

Ingredients

300g (10½oz) plain flour
2 teaspoons salt
4 tablespoons extra virgin
  olive oil
250ml (9fl oz) water

Method

Preheat the oven to 200°C (400°F), Gas Mark 6. Mix the flour and salt in a bowl, then add the oil and water and stir until a soft and sticky dough is formed. Add a little extra water if the mixture is too dry. Roll the dough out on a lightly floured surface.

Cut the dough into squares or rectangles (or whatever shape you desire!), transfer to a floured baking sheet and prick with a fork. Bake for around 15 minutes, until the edges are golden. Transfer to a wire rack to cool, then store in an airtight container.

Flour Tortillas

These can be really tricky to find without plastic packaging so I ended up making my own. I use them as wraps, filled with a spicy mixture of pulled pork and beans, or simply as a different way to serve up leftovers.

Ingredients
400g (14oz) self-raising flour
1 teaspoon salt
115g (4oz) butter, cut into little pieces
250ml (9fl oz) warm water

Method
Place the flour and salt in a bowl, add the butter and rub together with your fingertips until the mixture resembles breadcrumbs. Add the water to form a dough, then divide into balls, flatten and roll out on a lightly floured surface as thinly as possible. Cook the tortillas, one at a time, in a dry frying pan for about 30 seconds on each side.

Homemade Popcorn

This makes a really yummy and waste-free alternative to crisps, as popcorn kernels are among the easiest items to find in the bulk aisle. Homemade popcorn takes about five minutes to make and tastes amazing. I like to add salt and a drizzle of olive oil after cooking, or maple syrup, but feel free to get creative with different herbs and spices or melted chocolate... so many possibilities!

Ingredients
a little butter or oil
popcorn kernels

Method
Melt the butter or oil in a heavy-based saucepan, then throw in a handful or two of popcorn kernels. Cover with a lid and listen to them pop! Remove from the heat once the popping subsides, add your seasoning or flavouring of choice and enjoy.

YOGURT

If you don't have anyone selling yogurt in returnable, refillable or glass containers at a store or farmers' market then try this recipe. The live full-fat yogurt will act as a starter that can be used for every batch that you go on to make. Don't discard the whey as it is loaded with protein and you can add it to smoothies, mashed potato, scrambled eggs and pancakes. It's worth investing in some simple equipment such as a thermometer (borrow or find one second-hand).

Ingredients
1 litre (34fl oz) whole milk
120ml (4fl oz) live full-fat
  yogurt

Method
Gently heat the milk in a saucepan until it reaches 90°C (194°F). Take the pan off the heat and place it in a sink filled with an inch of cold water. Let cool until it reaches 45°C (113°F). Remove the pan from the cold water and stir in the live yogurt. Place a lid on the pan and store in a warm place (such as an insulated flask) overnight or for at least 8 hours.

If the consistency is too runny, place some cheesecloth inside a sieve and strain the yogurt to remove the excess liquid (the whey). Store the yogurt in a sterilized glass jar in the fridge and use within two weeks. Remember to keep half a cup (120ml / 4fl oz) aside as a culture for your next batch!

QUICK TIPS FOR USING UP ODDS AND ENDS

- **Leftover fruit and veg.** These can be added to smoothies, soups, sauces and stir-fries.

- **Save peelings and ends from carrots, onions, leeks and garlic.** Store these in the freezer to use for stock.

- **Beetroot tops.** Eat these instead of spinach or chard. Simply cook gently in butter or oil or throw into a stir-fry.

- **Cauliflower leaves.** Are often discarded but make a tasty snack. Simply coat in oil and spices and bake in the oven until crispy.

- **Pumpkin seeds make a delicious treat.** Toss in a bowl with melted butter, salt and spices and bake in the oven for 45 minutes at 150°C (300°F).

- **Offal and cheap cuts of meat.** These often go to waste, so try incorporating them into your meals from time to time – be adventurous!

- **Citrus peels.** Dry these in the oven and store. Use in cakes, teas and hot chocolate.

CLEANING

I love that my cleaning cupboard contains a few simple ingredients which can be mixed to make cleaning products as and when needed.

Here are a few simple ideas that you might find to be useful.

Repurpose and salvage storage jars and bottles. You will need plenty of reusable containers as well as refillable spray bottles.

Make extra and store. It is much easier and will be less time consuming in the long run if you make your cleaning products in bulk.

Simplify what you need. Do you really need lots of different products, each for an individual job? Try to use a multipurpose product instead.

Reduce your laundry. Air dry and spot clean your clothes.

If making your own isn't your idea of fun and you have access to a refill you like, then choose that instead. I do a bit of both. These are the recipes I have found most useful for keeping our home clean.

Basic All-Purpose Cleaning Spray

This is an effective and versatile spray which I use to disinfect surfaces around the home. I sometimes steep leftover citrus peels in a jar of vinegar for a week or more before diluting, to get a lightly fragranced version, and you could also experiment with herbs such as rosemary or eucalyptus leaves.

Ingredients
1 part distilled white vinegar
1 part water

Method
Mix equal quantities by volume of white vinegar and water and store in a glass or metal spray bottle.

How to use
Spray and wipe to disinfect and clean kitchen counters, sinks, fridges, door knobs, toys, tables, bathroom surfaces, windows, mirrors and glass. Don't use on granite or marble – see Disinfecting Vodka Spray on the right.

DISINFECTING VODKA SPRAY

Vodka makes a good alternative to vinegar and can be used safely on surfaces made from granite and marble (unlike vinegar). Try to buy it in a glass bottle. Neat vodka is also good for cleaning glass.

Ingredients
125ml (4fl oz) vodka
125ml (4fl oz) water
15 drops of essential oil
  of your choice (optional)

Method
Pour all the ingredients into a spray bottle and shake to mix.

How to use
Spray and wipe to disinfect kitchen and bathroom surfaces.

Washing Soda

For those who can't find it from bulk or in a cardboard box, here's how to make your own. I make several batches and store in glass jars, ready for making cleaning products.

Ingredients
Bicarbonate of soda
(baking soda)

Method
Simply sprinkle a thin layer (about 5mm/¼ inch deep) of bicarbonate of soda evenly onto a baking sheet and bake in the oven at 250°C (475°F), Gas Mark 9, for about an hour, stirring halfway through. When removing from the oven, notice how the texture is now more grainy and the colour duller and a little more grey than before. This is now washing soda, also known as soda crystals or soda ash. Store in an airtight container once cool.

How to use
This can be used to make various cleaning products, such as dishwasher powder and laundry powder (see right). You can also add 2 tablespoons to your laundry to soften water in hard-water areas.

LAUNDRY POWDER

I honestly recommend finding an eco-brand sold in bulk if you can, as the effectiveness of homemade laundry powder can vary, depending on the type of machine you have and the hardness of the water. It also takes a while to grate all that soap! But if you're keen to give it a go, here's how.

Ingredients

1 bar of castile soap, grated – about 100–150g (3½–5½oz)

1 x 250ml (9fl oz) cup borax substitute (bought in a cardboard box)

1 x 250ml (9fl oz) cup washing soda (see opposite)

Method

Mix together in a bowl and store in an airtight container.

How to use

Place 2 tablespoons in the powder draw of a 6kg (13lb) washing machine. Add more for a larger machine.

Dishwasher Powder

If you can't find plastic-free dishwasher tablets, or like to keep ingredients to a minimum, then try this. It takes no time to make and I have found it works very well.

Ingredients
4 parts washing soda
  (see page 202)
1 part citric acid
1 part sea salt

Method
Mix the ingredients together in a bowl and store in an airtight container.

How to use
Sprinkle into the tablet compartment and set to wash as normal. Use white vinegar as a rinse aid and adjust your machine to suit your local water hardness if possible. This last tip was a revelation for me! Read the manual and check online to find the hardness of your water supply.

Oven Cleaner

Goodbye harsh oven cleaners! Most shop-bought versions need serious ventilation and made my eyes water and throat sore, unlike this.

Ingredients
125ml (4fl oz) water
200g (7oz) bicarbonate
  of soda
1 tablespoon liquid castile
  soap or eco-friendly
  washing up liquid

Method
Mix the ingredients together in a bowl to form a paste.

How to use
Apply to the inside of the oven using a sponge or dish brush and leave for 30 minutes. Rinse thoroughly with warm water and wipe with a damp reusable cloth until the oven is completely clean.

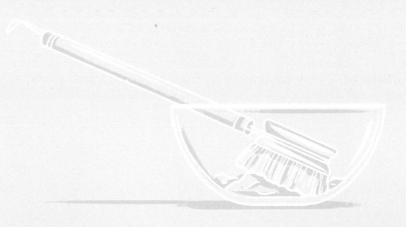

BEAUTY PRODUCTS

DIY beauty isn't essential and if you prefer to buy a ready-made product, then check the Resources section on page 215 or see what you have available locally.

Here are some tricks to get you started.

Think about what you use. Spend time working out what you need.

Keep or buy reusable metal or glass containers. You will need these for storage.

Swap it. If you can't find one of your favourite products in sustainable packaging, consider using a zero-waste alternative and be sure to contact the company to encourage them to make a change.

Minimize what you need. Could you use a multipurpose item? Often there is a single product that will work well.

Be smart. There are some products that you should always buy, and you cannot make an at home alternative. This includes sunscreen.

These are some of the recipes I have found to work well for my body. Remember, a little trial and error may be involved here.

Whipped Body Butter

This is a rich, moisturizing body butter which lasts a while. I like to use this straight after a shower. I sometimes use it on my face in the winter when my skin is extra-dry. For the carrier oil, try jojoba, apricot kernel oil, olive oil or sunflower oil.

Ingredients
125ml (4fl oz) shea butter
4 tablespoons carrier oil
10–15 drops of your
  favourite essential oil
  (optional)

Method
Whisk the ingredients together with a blender or electric hand whisk for several minutes (or longer if whisking by hand!) until it looks fluffy. Spoon the body butter into a glass jar and seal tight.

How to use
Simply massage onto the skin.

APPLE CIDER VINEGAR CONDITIONING HAIR RINSE

If you find your shampoo bar tends to leave a little residue behind in your hair, then this rinse helps to remove it and leaves hair feeling soft and conditioned.

Ingredients
1 part apple cider vinegar
5 parts warm water

Method
Mix the vinegar and warm water.

How to use
Pour the rinse through your hair, massage into the scalp then rinse thoroughly. If the smell of vinegar lingers, try diluting further. I tend to keep a jar of apple cider vinegar and an empty metal cup in the shower and simply measure it out there and then.

Clay Face Mask

This is a very simple face mask. Choose a clay to suit your skin type. Clays can be difficult to find in bulk, so look for one sold in a glass jar.

Ingredients
bentonite clay (or French green clay)
water

Method
Place enough clay for a face mask in a bowl and add water to form a paste. Avoid using a metal spoon or container as this can deactivate bentonite clay.

How to use
Massage onto the face and let it dry for 10–15 minutes. Remove with a warm, damp reusable face cloth.

ALL-PURPOSE BALM

I mostly use this as a lip balm but you can rub it into patches of dry skin or on your face when your skin feels dry. It can also be used to protect leather or as wood polish...it really is all-purpose! For the carrier oil, try sunflower or olive oil as they are easy to find in bulk. Jojoba, argan or almond oil may also be found in bulk or glass bottles.

Ingredients

1 tablespoon grated beeswax (I buy a large bar and grate it at home)
4 tablespoons carrier oil

Method

Combine the beeswax and carrier oil in a jar. Place the jar in a pan with a few centimetres (about an inch) of water and place over a medium heat. Once melted, pour the mixture into a small glass jar or metal tin and let it cool until solid.

How to use

Apply to dry lips, hands or any other areas that need a bit of moisture.

A FINAL NOTE

I sincerely hope this book has inspired you to reduce waste in your everyday lives. As you'll notice once you embark on this journey, there is still a lot to be done. Could you be a pioneer in helping to reduce unsustainable wasteful practices moving forward? Could you design a reusable or repairable product which you feel is missing from the market? If you have no access to a bulk store where you live, could you be the first to open one and get the community refilling and bringing their own containers? Maybe you are excellent at repairing electronics — try setting up a workshop with volunteers to teach others how to mend their things. Build a beauty brand based on refills! Whatever your passions are, use your skills to make a difference and help make waste-free living the more desirable choice. Be part of the new normal and be the change you want to see in the world.

Kate

RESOURCES

Eco-boost.co/shop – a curated collection of the items I use the most

Acalaonline.com – beauty and wellbeing products

Etsy.com – zero-waste and plastic-free beauty and cosmetics, as well as lifestyle products

Boobalou.co.uk – zero-waste lifestyle products

Lifewithoutplastic.com – zero-waste lifestyle products

Packagefreeshop.com – zero-waste lifestyle products

Buymeonce.com – specializes in eco-friendly and durable products. Most come with a lifetime warranty and repair service

Sinplastico.com – Spanish site offering zero-waste lifestyle products

Boutiquezerodechet.com – French site offering zero-waste lifestyle products

Biome.com.au – Australian site offering zero-waste lifestyle products

Greentulip.co.uk – ethical gifts and zero-waste lifestyle products

BABIES & KIDS

Funkymonkeypants.com – eco babywear and accessories

Thelittlegreensheep.co.uk – eco babywear and accessories

Realnappiesforlondon.org.uk – see the guide to reusable nappies

SECOND-HAND ITEMS

eBay.co.uk – buy and sell second-hand items (be sure to select 'auction' or 'used')

Gumtree.com – buy, sell or give away most things

Freecycle.org – collect or give away items for free

Olioex.com – collect or give away items for free, including leftover food

Vestiairecollective.com – pre-owned designer clothing and accessories

Oxfam.org.uk/shop – online charity shop

Amazon.co.uk – good for second-hand books

Depop – second-hand clothing app

CARBON FOOTPRINT CALCULATORS

Myclimate.org

Carbonfund.org

FIND BULK STORES NEAR YOU

App.zerowastehome.com
Thezerowastenetwork.com
Zerowastenear.me
Pebblemag.com/magazine/doing/plastic-free-shopping-13-of-the-uks-best-zero-waste-stores – list of UK zero-waste bulk stores

PLASTIC-FREE GROCERIES ONLINE (UK)

Zero-waste-club.com
Realplasticfree.com
PlasticFreePantry.co.uk
Organicdeliverycompany.co.uk/fruit-veg/produce-without-plastic.html
Loopstore.com – a circular shopping platform from Unilever and Terracycle offering a mixture of brands, some eco-friendly

PLASTIC-FREE TOILET ROLL

Whogivesacrap.org
Greencane.com
Hellotushy.com – bidet attachments

BEAUTY & PERSONAL CARE

Etsy.co.uk – search 'zero-waste makeup'
Acalaonline.com
Beautykubes.co.uk
Elatebeauty.com
Zaomakeup.co.uk
Fatandthemoon.com
Lamazuna.com
Plaineproducts.com
Scence.co.uk
Kindbeeuty.com
Packagefreeshop.com
Contentbeautywellbeing.com
Fairsquared.info/fairtrade-products-en/zero-waste/
Shethinx.com – period pants
Gladrags.com – period products
Mooncup.co.uk – menstrual cups

PETS

Scoopeasy.biz – paper dog pooper scoopers
Envirowagg.com/communities-with-solutions/ – towns with dog waste composting
Becopets.com – eco pet food and accessories

ZERO-WASTE RECYCLING BOXES

Terracycle.co.uk/en-GB/zero_waste_boxes

GUIDES

Sustainable clothing guide: eco-boost.co/
sustainable-style-guide/
Tips for setting up a bulk store:
Thezerowasteshop.co.uk/pages/zero-
waste/create-your-own-zero-waste-
shop/94
How to make a binliner from newspaper:
Instructables.com/id/How-to-Make-a-
Bin-liner-Our-of-Newspaper/
Food waste recipes: LoveFoodHateWaste.
com and Zerowastechef.com
How to make your own worm
composter: Youtube.com/
watch?v=JvUgdDZx66E&t=101s
Composting dog waste: https://www.nrcs.
usda.gov/Internet/FSE_DOCUMENTS/
nrcs142p2_035763.pdf

FIND A COMPOST SERVICE

Sharewaste.com
Findacomposter.com
Bootstrapcompost.com/residential-
service/
Compostnow.org/compost-services/

FILMS

Most of these can be found on Netflix or
rented online:
A Plastic Ocean
Bag It
A Plastic Tide
Tapped
The True Cost
Minimalism
RiverBlue
Soil Carbon Cowboys (on Vimeo)
Seed: The Untold Story
Before The Flood
An Inconvenient Truth
An Inconvenient Sequel

BOOKS

The Story of Stuff by Annie Leonard
Slow Death By Rubber Duck by Rick Smith
and Bruce Lourie
Simplicity Parenting by Kim John Payne
ToxIN ToxOUT by Rick Smith and Bruce
Lourie
A Life Less Throwaway by Tara Button
Zero Waste Home by Bea Johnson
Unprocessed by Megan Kimble
The Organically Clean Home by Becky
Rapinchuk

BLOGS

Zerowastehome.com
Trashisfortossers.com
GoingZeroWaste.com
Ecocult.com
Zerowastechef.com
Myplasticfreelife.com
Mamalina.co
Therogueginger.com
Sarahwilson.com
LeotieLovely.com

CHARITIES & DATABASES

Sas.org.uk (Surfers Against Sewage)
Mcsuk.org (Marine Conservation Society)
Plasticpollutioncoalition.org
Ellenmacarthurfoundation.org
Fashionrevolution.org
Soilassociation.org
Hubbub.org.uk
Wasteaid.org
Sustainablefoodtrust.org
Wrap.org.uk (Waste and Resources Action
  Programme)
Ewg.org/skindeep/
Recyclenow.com
Textileexchange.org
Loveyourclothes.org.uk/care-repair

REPAIR SPECIALISTS

iSmash.com
Clothes-doctor.com
Therestartproject.org
RepairCafe.org

RENT

Libraryofthings.co.uk
Renttherunway.com
Wearthewalk.co.uk
Rentuu.com
Zipcar.com
Girlmeetsdress.com

EVENTS

Paperlesspost.com
Greenvelope.com
Buyourhoneymoon.com
Patchworkit.com

TRAVEL

Loco2.com (trains and buses)
Footprint.wwf.org.uk
Carbotax.org

INDEX

advertising 122, 179
air conditioning 111
air travel 169–71, 174
alum stones 86
aluminium 21, 164
antibacterials 100, 106
apple cider vinegar 90, 209
art 142
asthma 94, 97

babies 175–9
bags
    plastic 49, 57
    reusable 9, 39, 67–8, 72, 74–8, 81, 173
Balm, All-purpose (recipe) 211
bathrooms 82–90
batteries 47
beach cleaning 139
beer, refills 49, 78, 164
'best before' dates 31
bicarbonate of soda 29, 86–8, 97, 103–4, 107, 202, 205
bills, paper-free 44
bin liners 54, 107
bin systems 50–4
body scrubs 90
bokashi bins 129–30
book reading 112–14
borrowing 16–17
bottle tops 49, 164
bottles
    glass 49, 69, 78, 164, 199
    reusable water 18–19, 39, 66–8, 72, 171–2
BPA 57
Bread Pudding (recipe) 189
bulk buying 27, 48–9, 74, 78–9, 81, 86–7, 90–1, 103, 173, 181
business cards 57, 156

campaigning 114, 142
camping trips 16–17, 173
candles 165
carbon footprint 174

cards 167
carpet freshener 103
catalogues 44
cats 182
celebrations 163–8
central heating 111
charity shops 120
chestnuts 109
children 175–9
Christmas 166–7
citric acid 105, 204
clay 90, 210
cleaning 96–114
cleaning products 29, 34, 79, 97–8, 100, 109
    Basic All-Purpose Cleaning Spray 101, 200
    Disinfecting Vodka Spray 101, 201
    natural 29, 97, 99, 101–4, 199–205
cleaning tools 49, 107
clothing 20, 37, 120, 135, 146–52, 176
cloths
    microfibre 107
    reusable 49, 70, 99, 107, 167
coffee 47, 70
composting 9, 23, 28, 124–31, 152, 156, 158, 164, 177, 180–2
confetti, natural 168
consumption 36
containers
    reusable 8, 9, 61, 67–9, 207
    see also cups, reusable; water bottles, reusable
cooking 30, 157
corks 164
cosmetics 29, 34, 61, 69, 82–3, 91–5, 172
    homemade 207–11
cotton 150
cotton buds 90
Crackers, Rustic (recipe) 193
Cradle to Cradle 150
crafting skills 72
cups 57
    reusable 66, 68, 73, 171
Custard (recipe) 190
cutlery 68, 155, 165, 171

decluttering 42, 115–23
decorations 166, 167, 168

deodorant 86
digital detoxes/decluttering 123
dishwashers 71, 101–2, 104–5, 202, 204
    Dishwasher Powder 204
disinfectants, natural 102
disposables 13, 18–19, 100, 107, 169–71, 173–4,
    177–8
documentaries 112–14, 161
dogs 181–2
downcycling 21
dry cleaning 99, 110

ear picks, reusable 69
eating out 157   9
educating others 52, 72, 81, 127, 155, 158, 160–2
egg cartons 77
electricity, saving 111
emails 111, 156
energy suppliers, green 44, 98, 109, 177
essential oils 106, 201, 208
events 163–8
example-setting 155

fabric softener 101
fabrics 150
face masks 90, 210
face washes 89–90
failure, feelings of 134–5
FairTrade 150
fairy lights 166
families 160–2, 175–9
fast fashion 37, 147, 151
'Five Rs' 14   24
    see also recycling; reducing; refusing; reuse; rot
fleas 182
floor cleaner 103
floss 89
flyers 57
food
    packaging 30, 31, 165, 187
    party 164
    pesticide residues 30
    and pets 181
    reusable containers for 67–9, 73–8, 80–1
    shopping 73–81
    and travel 171–3

unpackaged 28
food waste 9, 31, 54, 129–30, 157–8, 164, 187
    collections 23, 43, 45, 53, 131
freebies 57, 58, 156, 165
Freecycle 17

garage sales 120
gift wrap 167
gifts, experience-based 168, 179
glass
    bottles 49, 69, 78, 164, 199
    jars 67, 69–71, 76–8, 199
    recycling 21, 164
glitter, biodegradable 167
gloves, natural rubber 107
granite surfaces 101, 103
grooming 182
groups, zero-waste 62, 142

hair donations 95
hair dye 92
hair removal 88, 95
haircare products 87   8, 209
headphones 171
health issues 29–30, 100
hoarding 19, 117
home working 153
honey 89–90
horse chestnuts 12
hotels, eco 173
hygiene 71

jeans 20, 151
junk mail 45, 46

landfill 21
laundry 98–9, 101, 109, 151, 177, 199
    DIY laundry powder 12, 103–4, 202–3
leaflets 57
leather 150
leftovers 197
letter-writing 133, 136–8
libraries 44, 113, 179
limescale 102, 105
litter picking 133, 139
loofahs 12

magazines 44, 167
makeup remover 90
marble surfaces 101, 103
marketing lists 46
maternity clothing 176
meat-eating 35
medicines 94
menstrual cups 18, 68, 69, 71, 89
microbeads 95
microfibres, plastic 21, 107
milk deliveries 45
minimalism 36, 42, 87, 91–5, 153, 207
moisturizers 86, 208
money saving 28
moth repellents 99, 105
music streaming services 44

napkins 68, 99, 158, 165
nappies 177–8
newspapers 167
no-spend challenges 123

oils 86, 90, 106, 201, 208
olive oil 86, 90
online shopping 79
open register 46
organic textiles 150
oven cleaner 103, 205

packaging 8–9, 10–11, 59–60
contacting companies about 48, 136–8
cosmetics 95
food 30, 31, 165, 187
reusable 43
takeaways 159
and travel 169, 173
Pancakes (recipe) 191
paper 57, 156
parties 163–8
Pasta (recipe) 192
peelings 197
pens 153, 154
perfectionism 135
perfume 29
personal care 82–90, 95, 172
pesticide residues 30

petitions 114
pets 131, 180–3
phone directories 44
plasters 94
plastic 8, 9, 10
cutting down on 54, 55–8
lids 49
microfibres 21, 107
packaging 30, 173, 181
recycling 21
poo bags 181
Popcorn, Homemade (recipe) 195
possessions, reducing 16–17
printing 153

razors 69, 88
receipts 57
recipes 185–211
recycling 14, 21–2, 121
alternatives to 53
and bin systems 50–2
cards 167
children and 179
fabrics 21, 150, 152
keeping to a minimum 14
paper 156
and travel 172, 173
unusual items 53
reducing 14, 16–17, 19, 31, 45–6, 147, 157–8, 168, 181, 187, 199
refills 48–9, 59–61, 76, 78, 85–7, 89, 93, 95, 164
refusing 14, 15, 19, 55–8, 158, 170, 172, 179
renting 149, 168
repairs 14, 20, 48, 122, 151, 156
repurposing 152
research 59–62
responding 14, 24
reusables 57, 63–81
carting round 39, 75
cleaning 71
containers 8, 9, 61, 67–9, 207
cups 66, 68, 73, 171
and dry cleaning 99, 110
and eating out 157, 158
and entertaining 165
maternity 176

nappies 177–8
personal care 84–5, 89
and staying with other people 162
and travel 171–4
water bottles 18–19, 39, 66–8, 72, 171–2
for weddings 168
wipes 178
for the workplace 155
reuse 14, 18–19, 53, 156, 179, 183
rot 14, 23
see also composting
rust remover 102

sanitary ware 18, 68, 69, 71, 89
second-hand stuff 17, 37, 57, 117, 120–1, 148, 152,
  156, 166–8, 175, 178–9
selling stuff 120, 152
sharing economy 122
shaving cream/gel 49, 88
shopping 8–9, 32, 73–81, 122
showers 95, 111
skills, learning new 32, 33
soap 86, 89, 101–3, 105, 182, 203, 205
soap nuts 102
social media 136, 137
soil quality 35
solar panels 111
stain removal 105
stamps 156
statements, paper-free 44
stationery 154, 156, 168
sterilizing 71
stock (homemade) 188, 197
stores, zero-waste 59–60
straws 57, 68, 158
sunscreen 87, 172, 207
supermarkets 8–9
sustainability 149
synthetics 150

takeaways 30, 159
talks, organizing 140–1, 155
tare 27
tea-strainers 70
thinking ahead/planning 32
time management 32

tins, reusable 76–7
toilet roll 43, 45, 69, 89
toilet stain removal 105
toner 90
toothpaste/brushes 88–9
Tortillas, Flour (recipe) 194
toxoplasmosis 182
toys 179, 183
travel 169–74
trees 166

unpackaged options 59–60
up-to-date, keeping 62

vacuum cleaners 107
values 34
vegetables 79
vegetarians 35
video streaming services 44
vodka 99, 101, 201
volunteering 114

washing soda 104, 202–4
washing up liquid 102–3
water bottles, reusable 18–19, 39, 66–8, 72, 171–2
water saving measures 111
water-filters 171
weddings 168
Whipped Body Butter (recipe) 208
white vinegar 29, 49, 97, 99, 101–2, 107, 200
wine, refills 78, 164
wipes, disposable 100, 107, 178
workplaces 72, 142, 153–6
worm bins 23, 125, 127–9

Yogurt (recipe) 196
YouTube 7, 8, 141

zero-waste
  benefits 28–34
  definition 13
  'Five Rs' of 14–24
  groups 62, 142
  kit 63–81
  moving towards 25
  terminology 27

REFERENCES

1   https://www.pnas.org/content/114/23/6052

2   https://www.theguardian.com/environment/2013/jan/24/fish-channel-plastic-contamination

3   https://www.theguardian.com/lifeandstyle/2017/feb/14/sea-to-plate-plastic-got-into-fish

4   https://orbmedia.org/stories/Invisibles_plastics/multimedia and https://www.newscientist.com/article/dn28242-plastic-in-the-food-chain-artificial-debris-found-in-fish/ and https://www.theguardian.com/environment/2016/jun/20/microfibers-plastic-pollution-oceans-patagonia-synthetic-clothes-microbeads

5   https://assets.publishing.service.gov.uk/government/uploads/system/uploads/attachment_data/file/726926/expert-committee-pesticide-residues-food-annual-report-2017.pdf and https://www.newfoodmagazine.com/news/45901/nearly-half-british-foods-contain-pesticide-residue/

6   https://www.diabetes.co.uk/news/2017/jul/everyday-plastic-chemicals-linked-to-type-2-diabetes-risk-95492171.html

7   http://www.health.state.mn.us/divs/eh/indoorair/voc/ and https://iaqscience.lbl.gov/voc-svocs

8   https://www.wired.co.uk/article/receipt-recycling-uk-thermal-paper-digital-receipt

9   https://www.theguardian.com/science/2016/sep/02/antibacterial-soaps-banned-us-fda and http://sitn.hms.harvard.edu/flash/2017/say-goodbye-antibacterial-soaps-fda-banning-household-item/

10 https://www.eurekalert.org/pub_releases/2010-11/uom-sst112410.php and https://www.vox.com/2014/6/25/5837892/is-being-too-clean-making-us-sick and http://www.bbc.com/future/story/20151118-can-you-be-too-clean

11 http://www.ewg.org/guides/cleaners/content/cleaners_and_health#.WdW0mhNSyb8

12 https://www.huffingtonpost.co.uk/entry/how-to-fix-indoor-air-pollution_us_59e0cc85e4b03a7be58012b1 and https://www.epa.gov/indoor-air-quality-iaq/volatile-organic-compounds-impact-indoor-air-quality

13 https://brendid.com/green-cleaning-ingredients-you-should-never-mix/

14 https://www.fashionrevolution.org/dont-overwash-its-time-to-change-the-way-we-care/

15 http://www.energysavingtrust.org.uk/sites/default/files/reports/EST_11120_Save%20Energy%20in%20your%20Home_15.6.pdf

16 https://truecostmovie.com/learn-more/environmental-impact/

17 https://www.fashionrevolution.org/dont-overwash-its-time-to-change-the-way-we-care/

18 http://www.wrap.org.uk/sites/files/wrap/VoC%20FINAL%20online%202012%2007%2011.pdf

19 https://www.huffingtonpost.co.uk/entry/how-often-should-you-wash-denim-jeans_uk_5a5dca35e4b0fcbc3a130290

20 https://www.frasercoastchronicle.com.au/news/how-much-aussie-homes-really-waste-over-christmas/2881742/ and https://www.independent.co.uk/environment/how-to-stop-christmas-waste-and-the-thousand-of-tonnes-thrown-away-each-year-a7489766.html

21 http://www.apsnet.org/publications/apsnetfeatures/pages/christmastree.aspx

22 https://money.cnn.com/2010/12/16/news/economy/holiday_trash/index.htm

23 https://www.independent.co.uk/environment/disposable-nappies-a-looming-environmental-threat-477750.html

ACKNOWLEDGEMENTS

Firstly, I would like to thank my agent Zoe Ross for chasing me down and convincing me to write this book in the first place. Thank you for creating the opportunity and making it happen.

My husband, Mark, for his unrelenting belief in me and for supporting and joining me on my zero-waste journey.

My brother Matt, for the original idea of Six Weeks to Zero Waste.

My mother, Lesley, for her unwavering love and belief that I have something to offer the world. She may be a little biased...

My mother-in-law, Prudie, for her constant support and patience with my quirky zero-waste efforts!

My publisher Octopus, who completely understood my requests to make the production of this book greener than most and for their belief that I had a book in me. In particular, Stephanie – thank you for your enthusiasm for this book from the very beginning. Your energy is infectious, and I feel lucky to have your support

Bea Johnson, author of Zero Waste Home – thank you for inspiring me to live this lifestyle. I had the chance to interview Bea at a talk in Bristol and her passion for the zero-waste lifestyle is inspiring. She was warm, funny and a delight to spend time with. A true inspiration!

And finally, my YouTube and blog subscribers. Thank you for putting up with my sporadic upload schedule, terrible puns and amateur editing skills. I often receive messages that you were inspired to make some simple zero-waste changes after seeing one of my videos and honestly, that's all I ever wanted. Thank you for sharing your zero-waste journeys with me. They make me smile daily

For Mark, Arthur, Mum and Matt

An Hachette UK Company
www.hachette.co.uk

First published in Great Britain in 2019 by Gaia,
an imprint of
Octopus Publishing Group Ltd
Carmelite House
50 Victoria Embankment
London EC4Y 0DZ
www.octopusbooks.co.uk

Text Copyright © Kate Arnell 2019
Design and Layout Copyright © Octopus Publishing
Group Ltd 2019

Distributed in the US by
Hachette Book Group
1290 Avenue of the Americas
4th and 5th Floors
New York, NY 10104
www.octopusbooksusa.com

Distributed in Canada by
Canadian Manda Group
664 Annette St.
Toronto, Ontario, Canada M6S 2C8

ISBN 978-1-85675-411-8

A CIP catalogue record for this book is available
from the British Library.

Printed and bound in the Czech Republic

10 9 8 7 6 5 4 3 2 1

Publishing Director: Stephanie Jackson
Senior Editors: Leanne Bryan and Louise McKeever
Copy Editor: Joanna Smith
Art Director: Juliette Norsworthy
Designer: Rosamund Saunders
Illustrator: Abi Read
Senior Production Manager: Peter Hunt

The advice in this book is believed to be correct at the
time of printing, but the authors and the publishers
accept no liability for actions inspired by this book.

A NOTE ABOUT THE PRODUCTION
All the teams involved in the making of this book
have strived to reduce impact and have made efforts
to ensure the book is more environmentally friendly.
The paper used is FSC certified, the ink is vegetable-
based and the printer is low-carbon.